WORLD'S BEST BANK

PRAISE FOR *WORLD'S BEST BANK*

"Many leaders around the world are working through the challenge of how to digitally transform their organization. In Robin's new book he shares how DBS completely transformed every part of the organization and shows how all the different moving parts required for digitalization come together. I recommend reading this book for any leader involved in digital transformation to not only avoid common mistakes but also adopt best practices."

—Rita McGrath, Associate Professor, Columbia Business School; Best-Selling Author of *Seeing Around Corners*

"Understanding the human transformation underpinning the digital change interested me greatly, happy to see that Robin has ensured the voices behind the tools being used bring the change journey to life. A fascinating look behind the scenes of a leading digital transformation success story."

—Jean MacAskill, Corporate Team Coach, EMEAR, Cisco

"While the subtitle of the book is 'A Strategic Guide to Digital Transformation,' the book is in fact very human. Congratulations, Robin, for the detailed interviews conducted throughout the book's writing. You have done something amazing here, capturing the voices of so many in sharing the digital transformation journey of DBS, the world's best bank. I am sure many companies will benefit from the knowledge shared by the transformation talent in the book.

Robin has captured not just the importance of technology and talent to successfully transform the bank digitally, but also the importance of building trust among the leadership team and all employees, partners, and customers of the bank. This book allows you to hear the voices come alive in DBS's transformative journey."

—Annie Koh, Professor Emeritus of Finance (Practice), Lee Kong Chian School of Business, Singapore Management University

"This book will give leaders food for thought on their own organization's digital transformation. Although every transformation is unique, there are common lessons for everyone. Robin succeeds in transferring the energy and excitement of DBS digital transformation into every page of the book."

—Karen Lim, Managing Director, Digital Solutions, Standard Chartered Bank

"*World's Best Bank* skillfully narrates the transformation of DBS from a local bank to becoming the world's very best. With enjoyable page-turning style, this book takes you on a journey of hard-won insights and proven best practices to transform your organization from traditional to digitally driven. If you are—or want to become—a leader in digital transformation, you can clear the hurdles and avoid the pitfalls by applying Robin Speculand's real-world experience and advice."

—Ron Kaufman, *NY Times* Best-Selling Author and Global Customer Service Thought Leader

"Robin takes his lifelong pursuit of transformation success to the next level in this book. We've known for a long time that transformation is difficult under any circumstance. As the world becomes more connected, digital transformation requires that companies design and deliver strategies in a far more dynamic and responsive manner.

"Digital transformation is not just about digitizing what you have done in the past. It requires a nuanced understanding of the digital landscape within which you are operating and leveraging digital technologies to build the agility and responsiveness within your organization to maintain relevance within an ever-evolving digital ecosystem. Thankfully, Robin is here to show us how to do just that."

—Dr. Tony O'Driscoll, Fuqua School of Business, Duke University

"In an ever-changing, increasingly disruptive business environment, Robin's new book provides the intricate tools and success factors to develop a strategic road map for any company navigating its digital transformation journey. The DBS digital transformation success story sets a fantastic benchmark to aspire to—a must read for transformational business leaders."

—Ben Robinson, CEO, Raffles Quay Asset Management Pte Ltd

"Strategy implementation and digitalization specialist Robin Speculand brings to life the astonishing journey of the world's best bank, DBS, as it transformed its entire business through adopting digital. Robin's narrative is compelling and entirely relevant to the challenges many organizations are facing today. It acts as a practical how-to manual for those in the midst of their own transformational journey. In fact, it is the first book I have come across that explains how an entire business was transformed by leveraging digitalization.

"A unique, excellent piece of work and a must-read for business leaders and executive boards alike."

—Jeremy Blain, CEO, Performance Works International; Author of *The Inner CEO: Unleashing Leaders at All Levels*

"Organizations and especially airlines are currently being challenged. One of these critical challenges is how they deal with digitalization. Robin has written the definitive strategic guide based on the story and lessons from DBS Bank. I recommend all leaders read it."

—Shashank Nigam, Founder & CEO, SimpliFlying

"Robin is deeply passionate about strategy implementation and about helping leaders and organizations benefit from best practices. Through this lens, he captures DBS's compelling transformation story and offers a clear articulation of its building blocks."

—Marvin Tan, Senior Executive in Singapore

"Humankind has used great and captivating stories over millennia, to distill wisdom and amplify insight. In the world of business, what DBS has achieved over its recent history is one such example. To me, it is this story of banking reinvented, coupled with the captivating storytelling of Robin Speculand, which makes this book a very compelling read."

—Gyan Nagpal, Best-Selling Author of *Talent Economics* and *The Future-Ready Organization*

WORLD'S BEST BANK: A Strategic Guide to Digital Transformation

For further information, contact bridges@bridgesconsultancy.com.

Published by Bridges Business Consultancy Int
www.worlds-best-bank.com

First Edition
Printed in Singapore

ISBN: 978-981-18-0918-7 (Hardback)
ISBN: 978-981-18-0919-4 (Paperback)
ISBN: 978-981-18-0920-0 (Ebook)

This book is dedicated to the world's best wife, GraceKelly.

Contents

Introduction 13

Author's Profile 17

Chapter 1 The Battle Cry from the Beach. 19

Chapter 2 Three Strategic Waves Introduction . . . 25

Chapter 3 The Asia Wave 33

Chapter 4 The Digital Wave 43

Chapter 5 First Strategy Principle of Digital Wave: Become Digital to the Core 49

Chapter 6 Changing Technology's DNA 58

Chapter 7 Best Practices for Becoming Digital to the Core 62

Chapter 8 Second Strategy Principle of Digital Wave: Embed Ourselves in the Customer Journey. 71

Chapter 9 Putting Our Customer at the Heart of Everything We Do 73

Chapter 10 Customer Journey Examples. 84

Chapter 11 Building Ecosystems 104

Chapter 12 Ecosystems Examples. 113

Chapter 13 Customer Trust. 122

Chapter 14 Third Strategy Principle of Digital Wave: Culture by Design, and Think Like a Start-up 128

Chapter 15 Adopting Agile. 135

Chapter 16 Be a Learning Organization. 146

Chapter 17 Customer Obsessed 155

Chapter 18 Data-Driven Culture 161

Chapter 19 Experiment and Take Risks 178

Chapter 20 The Sustainability Wave 188

Chapter 21 Covid-19 Pandemic Response 201

Appendix

A. *World's Best Bank* Platform 213

B. Strategy Implementation Institute. 218

C. Award-Winning Bank 220

D. Glossary 222

Acknowledgments 225

"You don't want a digital strategy.
You want a strategy for the digital world."

— Robin Speculand

Introduction

The first time I published details about the remarkable transformation happening in DBS Bank was 2017 in my book *Excellence in Execution*. Piyush Gupta, CEO of DBS Group, thoughtfully wrote the foreword for that book. The digital transformation of DBS Bank was included as a successful case study of strategy implementation (my field of specialty). I had also published the first of two case studies about the bank with Singapore Management University. At that time, the bank had just won the inaugural World's Best Digital Bank award from *Euromoney* magazine.

But that was only a hint at what was to come!

My challenge has been to capture this exceptional digital transformation in the pages of this book. In *World's Best Bank*, I reflect the passion and intricacy that drove the bank's transformation to become the world's best, while providing a strategic guide to digital transformation for you.

You will discover how DBS transformed its culture, employees, technology, operations, business and even its customers. You will also understand how, today, the bank continues striving to become a technology organization.

World's Best Bank is for leaders responsible for digital transformation who want to learn and benchmark themselves against world-class digital transformation. As you will read, I dive deeply into the areas required for your digital transformation, and I recommend focusing on those most relevant to you. For example, the deep dive into re-architecture of technology may not be as relevant to you as the deep dive into adopting design thinking for the customer.

My connection with Piyush began when we both worked at Citigroup in the 1990s. After he assumed stewardship of DBS Bank in 2009, I consulted to the bank as it successfully implemented its **Asia Wave** strategy, the first of three strategies he initiated.

The second strategy was the **Digital Wave**, which is what this book concentrates on. Given that about two-thirds of digital transformations succeed, I have highlighted the bank's lessons, best practices, and secrets for success that you can adopt for your own transformation. Following each of the three sections that explain specific strategic principles, you will find Questions for Consideration to enhance your own digital transformation.

I started researching for the book at the end of 2018. In early 2020, I had just completed writing this manuscript when the world changed dramatically. I postponed the book's publication to detail how the bank has responded to the Covid-19 pandemic and its third strategy—the **Sustainability Wave**.

Throughout this book, you'll see how the bank's transformation came to life through its experiences and stories. You'll also discover how it overcame hurdles that trip up so many organizations, while sharing best practices you can readily bring into your organization.

In becoming the World's Best Bank, DBS achieved these innovative "firsts":

- Became the first bank in the world to hold all three prestigious Best Bank in the World titles within a 12-month period—from *Euromoney*, *The Banker*, and *Global Finance*. (In the banking world, this is the equivalent of a movie winning three Oscars—for best movie, best director, and best actor.)
- Became the first bank to identify how to capture the value of digitalization on its scorecard.
- Won the first digital bank award from *Euromoney* in 2016.
- Launched the world's largest open banking API platform in 2017.
- Opened the world's first online treasury and cash management simulation platform.
- Launched the world's first in-school savings and payment program using wearable technology in 2017.

DBS Bank was recognized by *Harvard Business Review* in 2019 as one of the top 20 business transformations of the past decade. Piyush has also been named in HBR's 2019 edition of "The CEO 100," HBR's annual list of the world's top chief executives.

It's been a delight researching and narrating DBS Bank's success story. Opinions expressed in this book are solely my own and are not attributable to DBS, its staff, affiliates, or other groups or individuals.

To support your digital transformation, the book is part of a platform experience offering a variety of implementation support that can be viewed in the appendix or on the book's landing page - www.worlds-best-bank.com.

I hope the enthusiasm of this remarkable journey comes across on these pages for you. Most of all, I hope it guides you to create a successful transformation in your own organization.

Robin Speculand,

Global Pioneer in Strategy
& Digital Implementation

Author's Profile

ROBIN SPECULAND

Strategy & Digital Implementation Specialist

Robin Speculand passionately lives and breathes strategy implementation. He continually creates new approaches to support leaders in transforming their organizations and is one of the world's most prolific writers on the subject.

Robin has founded three companies, three business associations, and is the CEO of Bridges Business Consultancy Int. Singapore Airlines was among the first organizations to embrace this new field and engage Robin to support its global strategy implementation.

He is known for his breakthroughs on implementation methodology and techniques, including the *Implementation Compass*™, a proprietary framework built on the eight areas for excellence for execution; *Readiness2Execute Assessment*; *Ticking Clock© Model*, a framework for digitalizing an organization;

Digital Maturity Index, a self-assessment that reveals a person's level of digital maturity; and the 40 Digital Best Practices Benchmark.

Robin also co-founded an online education forum—the *Strategy Implementation Institute*—that provides leaders with a community, online course, and online certification in the field.

In 2014, Robin recognized that digital transformation was markedly different and presented new challenges. He researched the challenges globally and in 2018 co-authored the white paper *Transforming Your Company into a Digital-Driven Business*. In 2021 he co-authored the white paper *The Future of Strategy Implementation*.

In 2021 Robin was co-nominated with Piyush Gupta, CEO of DBS Bank, for the Thinkers50 "Ideas into Practice Award" and was the winner of the "Business Strategist" Singapore 2021–22 by Prestige.

Robin has published five books on strategy implementation. His latest, *World's Best Bank—A Strategic Guide to Digital Transformation*, is an Amazon best seller. His pioneering work has been featured in media worldwide, including BBC World and *Forbes*. He is a TEDx speaker and an educator for Duke CE, IMD, and an adjunct member of Singapore Management University and National University of Singapore. He is an award-winning and Harvard listed case writer and a GlobalScot appointed by the First Minister of Scotland.

Outside of work, Robin competes in Ironman events around the world and calls Singapore home.

CHAPTER 1

The Battle Cry from the Beach

Piyush took to the stage in Phuket, Thailand, to share his new vision for DBS Bank. It's 2014, and the CEO of DBS had brought his leadership team together to recognize the bank's successes and catalyze the launch of a new strategy.

Piyush joined DBS as group CEO in late 2009. In 2010, his leadership team launched a new strategy called the Asian Bank of Choice for the New Asia. This five-year strategy didn't focus on being either a leading domestic bank or an international bank. Rather, it aimed to occupy the sweet spot between the two while increasing its standards to operate at international banking standards. Remarkably, this five-year strategy was implemented 12 months ahead of schedule.

Piyush opened his speech on the beach in Phuket by reflecting on the bank's successes under his stewardship. By 2014, it had achieved all of its key targets: 1) voted Asian Bank of Choice for the New Asia, 2) ranked top for customer service, 3) received an innovation award for cutting-edge technology, and 4) recognized as a thought leader of Asia.

But this was just the beginning. Before the retreat, Piyush had met with Jack Ma, then CEO of Alibaba. That intriguing one-hour meeting convinced him of the potential disruptive cyclone emerging out of China and changing the way banking was being conducted. That instilled in him the need for a new strategy in order for DBS to compete in the changing strategic digital landscape.

The bank's annual board meeting had just been held in South Korea. At that time, South Korea was a leader in using mobile applications and providing leading-edge technology. Board members and leaders took time on this visit to identify how mobile could be better applied to banking.

In addition, the success of being voted Asian Bank of Choice encouraged DBS leaders to be more aggressive in deciding what their new strategy could achieve. They also could see turbulent times ahead. As a result, they set a "big, hairy audacious goal"—to become the Best Bank in the World (BBIW) by March 2020.

From the stage in Phuket, Piyush held up the masthead of a mockup article stating, "DBS is the best bank in the world." To achieve this goal meant not copying other banks' performance. Instead, it called for a battle cry that would drive every employee toward this aggressive vision. It required creating and implementing a powerful strategy to differentiate the bank from its competitors. For DBS, this meant changing

To achieve this goal meant not copying other banks' performance. Instead, it called for a battle cry that would drive every employee toward this aggressive vision.

its customers' perception of banking as a chore to Making Banking Joyful—the new battle cry.

Making Banking Joyful

The DBS leaders recognized that "money lubricates life" is a powerful statement. But the team also recognized that this saying could quickly become prosaic—too ordinary. That's because people tend to take banking for granted or even see it as a negative in their lives. So, the leaders strived to identify what "banking with a sense of purpose" would be like.

After the global financial crises in 2008, many people started distrusting banks and even called banking "painful." Research at the time indicated that 71 percent of people preferred having root canal surgery over dealing with a bank![1] The question the leaders addressed was not "what does the bank want to do?" but "how do we make dealing with DBS easy, fun, convenient, and meaningful?" Then people would be able to see the kind of good the bank did for businesses and individuals as well as the value it added to society.

The question the leaders addressed was not "what does the bank want to do?" but "how do we make dealing with DBS easy, fun, convenient, and meaningful?"

The team migrated toward making banking the opposite of painful—that was, to Making Banking Joyful.

At the time of the Phuket meeting, several significant and relevant strategic global changes were occurring. These included

1 Dan Kadlec, "Why Millennials Would Choose a Root Canal Over Listening to a Banker," Time.com, March 28, 2014, https://time.com/40909/why-millennials-would-choose-a-root-canal-over-listening-to-a-banker/.

numerous new entrants who were "unbundling" banking; rising customer expectations from the use of new technologies; vendor-managed tech stack becoming exceedingly costly; the rise of globalization platform giants such as Tencent and Alibaba in the East, and Google and Amazon in the West.

Due to the emergence of numerous technologies, the means for Making Banking Joyful was rapidly evolving. DBS leaders recognized that, by leveraging these new technologies, they could make banking "invisible" to their customers. That would, in turn, create opportunities for customers to have enjoyable interactions when dealing with the bank and, ultimately, to experience a sense of happiness and peace of mind throughout their banking journey.

DBS leaders recognized that, by leveraging these new technologies, they could make banking "invisible" to their customers.

Four Themes

In launching the Making Banking Joyful strategy, these four themes underpinned the bank's transformation effort:

1. The transformation agenda needed to be driven by a purpose. At DBS, Making Banking Joyful took hold at the root of how everyone at the bank would think and act. It inspired and drove every part of the bank to take the right actions to implement the strategy.
2. Digital transformation is not only about technology; it's about both the hardware of technology and its software—that is, *people* transformation. Both require hard work, and the bank had to consider elements such as its

customers' experience, its organization's culture, and its desired way of working. Today, balancing the hardware and the software is a recognized transformation success factor, but in 2014, it was not.

3. DBS digitally transformed its whole organization from the start. At the time, many organizations began digitization with one division or had a skunkworks project (a small group of people working outside of the main business on a project innovation). DBS bet on the *whole* organization transforming, believing that both older and younger employees could master the change. As Piyush pointed out, older people didn't need to be slow in adopting new technologies. Because they are constantly changing in their personal lives, they can also change in their professional lives. Thus, with everyone dealing with change equally, the bank avoided creating a chasm between the younger and older employees.

4. Business is technology; technology is business. In DBS, there is no more front-, middle- and back-office divisions. That is yesterday's language. Today's language is *one bank serving the customer in an integrated manner.* Breaking down the silos between front-, middle- and back-office is a major transformation in the traditional way a bank operates.

Today's language *is one bank serving the customer in an integrated manner.*

Early Recognition – Winning Best Digital Bank in the World in 2016

As early as 2016, DBS became recognized for its digital transformation progress.

Being awarded the world's best digital bank by *Euromoney* magazine was a surprise to many in DBS. At that time, the leaders considered the bank to be "cutting edge" but not yet necessarily the best. The award recognized the bank's journey and harnessed everyone's energy toward its shared vision and objectives. It also turned into a wonderful morale booster, which made the transformation process easier to continue.

In 2018, two years ahead of schedule, the bank achieved its battle cry from BBIW Phuket and received global recognition as the Best Bank in the World. DBS became the only bank in the world to concurrently hold three of the most prestigious best bank awards from *The Banker*, *Global Finance*, and *Euromoney* in a 12-month period.

DBS has been voted the "Best Bank in the World" for three years running in multiple publications.

CHAPTER 2

Three Strategic Waves Introduction

To explain the bank's strategic focus under Piyush's stewardship, DBS refers to the Three Waves: Asia, Digital, and Sustainability.

The inter-relationship among the three strategic waves was critical to the bank's success. Throughout the implementation of each wave, DBS leaders were diligent in assuring they had the right measures in place to track performance and inspire employees to implement them.

The Asia Wave (2010–2014)—to become the Asian Bank of Choice for the New Asia—improved the way the bank operated, caught the wave when China was opening up, and partially laid the foundation for the Digital Wave that followed.

The Digital Wave (2015–2018)—to bet on and catch a Digital Wave that would make banking joyful. The success of this wave is the main focus of this book.

The Sustainability Wave (2019–forward)—to address issues of inequality, new social norms, and the future of our planet as they become increasingly crucial.

DBS Scorecard

The bank adopted a Balanced Scorecard to set objectives, drive behaviors, measure performance, and determine remuneration during the implementation of each strategic wave.

Measuring the Asia Wave

During the implementation of the Asia Wave, the DBS Balanced Scorecard was comprised of traditional KPIs in three categories:

1. *Shareholder* metrics focused on achieving sustainable growth and measured financial results. KPIs included income growth, expense-related ratios, and return on equity. The bank also measured risk-related KPIs to ensure the DBS Group's income growth was balanced against the level of risk taken. Control and compliance KPIs were also a focus in this section.
2. *Customer* metrics focused on positioning DBS as a bank of choice. These measures included the bank's achievement in increasing customer satisfaction, depth of customer relationships, and brand positioning.
3. *Employee* metrics focused on positioning DBS as an employer of choice. These measures included employee engagement, training, mobility, and turnover.

The strategic priorities, also on the Scorecard, set out the initiatives the bank intended to complete within 12 months.

As part of its long-term journey toward achieving its strategic objectives, it set specific KPIs and targets for nine priorities and other areas of focus.

Measuring the Digital Wave

Early in the implementation, the bank had to find ways to measure the value of digital transformation. Also, when the bank started implementing the Digital Wave, the leadership team realized it could not demonstrate to analysts or shareholders the value that came from having digital customers.

The team focused on figuring out the difference between customers who were digitally active and those who were not. They predicted that the bank would realize improved outcomes from a revenue, expense, and returns perspective from its digitally active customers compared with its non–digitally active customers. To confirm this conjecture required adopting new measures to track customers' digital activities. This led to DBS becoming the first bank in the world to identify *how to capture digital value creation*.

Over the first three years of the Digital Wave, the team demonstrated that when customers became digitally active—that is, they conducted more than half of their banking activities digitally—their total engagement with the bank went "through the roof." The number of times they checked their balance, the number of payments they made, and the number of physical activities they did all increased. In fact, depending on whether it was an individual or SME (Small Medium Enterprise) customer, the number of activities increased to 16 times or even as many as 60 times.

Impressively, the total amount of business from SME customers more than doubled during that three-year period. Even more impressive was that, overall, digital customers created *double* the income of traditional customers.

> Even more impressive was that, overall, digital customers created *double* the income of traditional customers.

At the same time, with everything starting to be digitized, the cost of processing decreased. The bank focused on creating Straight-Through Processes or STP. (Note: Various terms such as STP are explained in the glossary found in this book's appendix.) In 2020, the cost-income ratio of the digital segment was 30 percentage points below the traditional segment, with the differential widening from 20 percentage points in 2019.[2]

During the implementation, visible results and rapid investment payback inspired and sponsored more activities. Various activities helped convert more non-digital customers into digital customers. By the end of 2020, 75 percent of all interactions across the bank were handled digitally. In part, this number increased due to the effect of the Covid-19 pandemic and people staying home.

The bank also recognized that the value of digitalization is greater on the revenue line than the expense line. They also discovered that customers find dealing with the bank digitally more convenient than doing so in person. This increased the "share of wallet" measure. The convenience of banking digitally caused a shift in customers' mindsets similar to shopping online. It's human nature; once

> The bank also recognized that the value of digitalization is greater on the revenue line than the expense line.

2 "Annual Report 2020," DBS, accessed April 16, 2021, page 14, https://www.dbs.com/annualreports/2020/index.html?pid=sg-group-pweb-investors-pdf-2020-stronger-together.

people start buying or banking online, the process becomes easier, so they do it more often.

Tom or Dave

Rather than constantly calling customers "traditional" or "digital" (T or D), the bank adopted the names "Tom" for traditional and "Dave" for digital customers. Dave customers are defined by their activities within the most recent 12 months:

- Made a product purchase or segment upgrade via digital channel
- Completed more than 50 percent of financial transactions via digital channel
- Conducted more than 50 percent of non-financial transactions via digital channels

By comparison, Tom customers prefer traditional banking practices. (In measuring these, the bank excludes transactions that don't represent a preference of either traditional or digital behavior such as ATMs or credit card transactions due to their ubiquitous nature.)

To understand this traditional customer banking behavior, the bank developed tools to study the data. In addition, it wanted to make sure the change in behavior from Tom to Dave was sustainable, so it put into place a criterion to measure this behavior over a rolling 12-month period. During that time, if Dave stopped demonstrating digital behaviors, he became a Tom.

This practice incentivized all the businesses to ensure they focused on acquiring new Daves as well as converting Toms to Daves—and keeping their business.

Acquire, Transact, Engage – ATE

In 2015, every part of the business started developing its own way of creating and measuring digital initiatives. This led to leaders assigning an ATE acronym—Acquire, Transact, Engage—to the Digital Wave to ensure conformity in the measurement. ATE means:

Acquire – Measure the progress in leveraging digital channels to acquire new customers and grow digital channel share.

Transact – Measure the progress in eliminating paper and driving automation to deliver instant fulfillment.

Engage – Measure the progress in driving customer engagement, conversion, and contextual marketing cross-buy across their digital assets.

ATE became known throughout the bank as the Big Tech Model.

Ecosystems Added – EATE

With the launch of the API platform in 2017, "E" was added to the ATE scorecard to track the performance of ecosystems. This four-part scorecard measured progress made on growing and developing meaningful relationships with the bank's ecosystem partners.

Balanced Scorecard and Annual Report

DBS includes its Balanced Scorecard in its annual report, so by default, it also shares its strategy. The bank leaders strongly believe the differentiator is not just having a strategy but having a strategy that's well implemented. This is when the whole organization comes together to focus on the customer and embraces the new mindset, culture, and direction. The Balanced Scorecard has already set the goals, targets, and actions to implement the strategy into the bank's various businesses and departments.

Every year, the Balanced Scorecard is updated by the end of December so each business can start delivering on its target by January 1st. The scorecard must be approved by the board before being cascaded throughout the organization. Its purpose is to ensure the goals of every business, country, and support function are aligned across the bank.

The Value of the Digital Wave

Over the years, these major insights have emerged from the bank's Balanced Scorecard:

- Income earned from a typical digital customer is more than twice that from a typical traditional customer. Digital customers increased from 3.3 million in 2019 to 3.7 million in 2020.
- Digital customers grew from 33% of the bank's base in 2015 to 78% in 2020.
- The cost-income ratio differential between digital and traditional customers widened to 30 percentage points in 2020 from 20 percentage points in 2019. Digital customers conduct 16 times or even as many as 60 times more transactions, have higher balances in accounts, and enjoy higher overall engagement than traditional customers.
- The return on equity from digital customers is 32%, which is 10 percentage points higher than the return on equity from traditional customers.

- In 2017, DBS Group's net profit rose 4% to $4.39* billion. In 2018, its net profit rose 28% to $5.63 billion. In 2019, its net profit rose 14% to $6.39 billion. In 2020, DBS Group's net profit was $4.72 billion.
- In 2020, total income remained stable at $14.6 billion. The bank's early investment in digital transformation and the shift to being a purpose-driven bank supported its operations through this challenging year.
- Despite the year's challenges, 2020 saw the bank record its highest-ever operating performance of $8.43 billion. This reflected the strength of the franchise and its excellence in execution.

**All numbers in this book are in Singapore dollars.*

CHAPTER 3
The Asia Wave

In 2010, just a few months after joining the bank, Piyush took his top leaders on a three-day retreat to craft a new strategy. The strategy that came out of this 2010 retreat covered three main areas:

1. Asian Bank of Choice for the New Asia – What the bank wanted to be
2. Nine Strategic Priorities
3. Five Asian Pillars – Principal areas of differentiation and competitive advantage

1. Asian Bank of Choice for the New Asia

The strategy identified how DBS would be the Asian Bank of Choice for the New Asia. Not a domestic bank and not an international bank, it would occupy the sweet spot between the two. From that emerged a vision of an Asian bank that differed from local lenders or global players.

By specializing in Asia, DBS would have the reach and sophistication to outcompete local lenders. Its deep Asian insights distinguished the bank from its global competitors.

"New Asia" was a forward-looking statement of what the bank thought Asia was turning out to be—that is, more sophisticated and confident about itself. But the bank also did not want to lose sight of the values that made Asia special.

Leaders also agreed that DBS had to be strong at home. How could it be known as a strong Asian bank without dominating the Singapore market?

2. Nine Strategic Priorities

At the retreat, the leadership team identified strategic priorities in three distinct areas:

Geographies

1. Entrench its position in Singapore.
2. Reposition the Hong Kong franchise.
3. Rebalance the geographic mix of the business.

Regional businesses

4. Build a leading SME banking business across the region.
5. Strengthen the wealth proposition across the region to better serve the increasing number of potential new clients.

Enablers

6. Build the Global Transaction Services (GTS) and treasury customer business across the region.
7. Place customers at the heart of the DBS banking experience.

8. Focus on management processes, people, and culture.
9. Strengthen the technology and infrastructure platform.

These priorities then formed the basis of the group's scorecard.

"Banking the Asian Way" was woven throughout the strategy and became the differentiator when defining relationships with customers and employees. The strategy also allowed the bank to provide unique Asian insights and design solutions for its customers while enjoying seamless connectivity across a network of key Asian markets.

3. Five Asian Pillars

How the bank would differentiate itself became known as the five Asian pillars.

1. Asian Relationships – DBS strives to embody the elements of what relationships are about in Asia. We recognize that relationships have swings and roundabouts. We look at relationships holistically, recognizing that not every transaction needs to be profitable in its own right. We stay by our clients through down cycles.
2. Asian Service – DBS service ethos is built on the RED motto: being Respectful, Easy to deal with, and Dependable, with the humility to serve and the confidence to lead.
3. Asian Insights – DBS knows Asia better than others; we provide unique Asian insights and create bespoke Asian products. Our customer conversations are underpinned by award-winning research that offers insights into markets and industries in Asia.
4. Asian Innovation – DBS constantly innovates new ways of banking that are appropriate to our markets as

we strive to make banking faster, more intuitive, and more interactive.

5. Asian Connectivity – DBS works in a collaborative manner across geographies, supporting our customers as their numbers expand across Asia.

This strategy was presented to the board of directors for approval. The board backed the leadership team and approved opening up to challenges such as developing trade in China and a new technology infrastructure. The board acknowledged that this effort required a higher risk appetite and greater investment than before.

DBS Bank launched its new strategy in Shanghai in 2010 when opening its new office there. This event emphasized the bank's new regional focus. Strategies and priorities were shared with the analysts and, as they were implemented, the results were linked back to the strategic objectives.

The bank's leaders became clearer on what success for DBS would look like, what it would take to achieve the strategic outcomes, how to sequence the outcomes, and what would need to be measured. The new strategy and Piyush's stewardship brought stability, which led to results. In addition, the new strategy launch gave employees an opportunity to create something different over the next few years. They rose to the occasion.

Global Financial Crisis

What made crafting and implementing the strategy in 2010 even more challenging was seeing the world emerge from the global financial crisis. It was an uncertain time in the banking industry, which was undergoing a profound change itself. Regulators worldwide had tightened standards to remove excesses from riskier aspects of the business and to limit speculative activities. Pressure from communities to steer banking back to more traditional and genuinely useful activities was building.

In response, the banking industry underwent a perceptible shift from *expediency* to *values* and from *short-term profit maximization* to *long-term profit sustainability*. Instead of creating banking products that turned toxic, it shifted to products that facilitated the production of economic goods and services. DBS also responded to increasing demands for enhanced reporting to better demonstrate their commitment to corporate governance and responsibility to multiple stakeholders. This would later affect DBS's leaders when launching the Sustainability Wave across the bank.

Other changing trends affecting banks included analytics, technology, and customer behavior. In addition, mobile banking was the fastest-growing area of contact between customers and the bank.

Best Practices from Implementing the Asia Wave

DBS Bank successfully implemented the Asia Wave by achieving all the key strategic goals 12 months ahead of the five years anticipated. Some best practices allowed the bank to be successful when, at that time, two-thirds of organizations were failing at implementation (as per Bridges Business Consultancy Int research[3]). Five best practices included:

---

3 "Research and Case Studies," Bridges Consultancy, accessed April 12, 2021, http://www.bridgesconsultancy.com/research-case-study/research.

Best Practices #1: RED

During the 2010 leadership meeting, the team spent two days defining what Asian Service (one of the five pillars of the strategy) meant to the bank. The outcome was the acronym RED, which stands for:

- **R**espectful
- **E**asy to deal with
- **D**ependable

RED (also the bank's branding color) made the concept of *Asian Service* real to DBS employees. It was something they could translate into their own work.

To oversee the RED activities and ensure an alignment of events, the Customer Experience Council (CEC), chaired by Piyush, was established. The fact that Piyush chaired this council sent a powerful message throughout the bank on the importance of RED and the new strategy.

Looking back, DBS Bank had the worst service in Singapore in 2010, as measured independently by the Customer Satisfaction Index of Singapore (CSISG). Through RED initiatives, employees felt empowered to make changes—and make a difference—that drove their customers' experience in positive ways. Four years later, DBS Bank was rated the best in customer satisfaction, even higher than Singapore Airlines, the company which it ironically had benchmarked against to learn about customer service. In fact, "RED" had become an active verb for the way people worked, just as people say "Google" for search or "FedEx" for delivery.

More information on how the bank implemented the Asia Wave is available in the case study I published in collaboration with Singapore Management University.[4]

Figure 1.0 is a graphic display of how customer satisfaction increased over time.

Figure 1.0: Singapore Management University's Annual Customer Satisfaction Survey, with permission

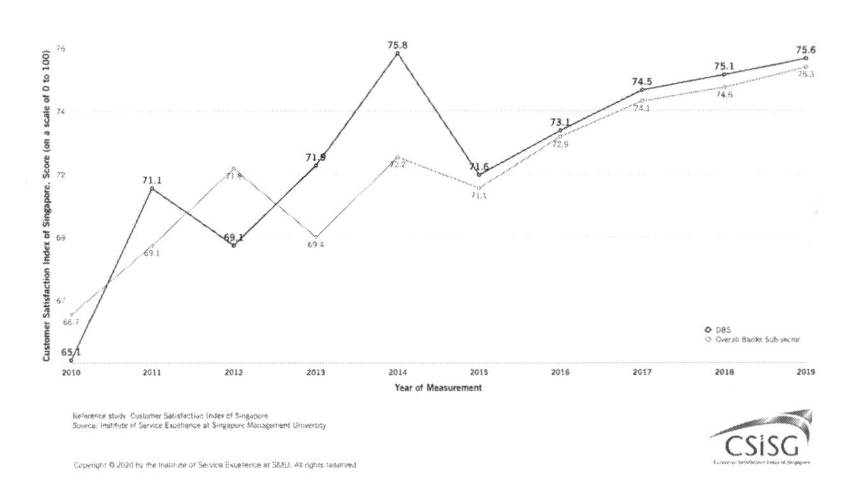

Best Practices #2: RED in the Digital Age

RED helped prepare the groundwork for digitalization. In 2017, the bank's leaders revisited what RED would mean in the digital age. "Respectful" initially described how the bank wanted employees to treat each other and their customers. Today, this word means more. For example, it refers to respecting a customer's cell phone battery life and data package (e.g., they don't want to ask customers to upload something that burns through

4 Robin Speculand and Adina Wong, "DBS Bank: Transformation through strategy implementation," July 2016, https://ink.library.smu.edu.sg/cases_coll_all/159.

their data package). "Easy to deal with" initially focused on eliminating customer hours and fixing the "plumbing." Today, it also means having great user interfaces and experiences. "Dependable" initially focused on reliability. Today, it also means high performance of the bank's systems.

RED continues to evolve as it drives the right behaviors of employees and enables DBS to differentiate itself from other banks in its service to customers.

Best Practices #3: PIE

Before Piyush joined DBS, the bank had launched Process Improvement Events (PIE). PIE was an approach for a team to redesign a process that needed improving. Over five days, they would identify the process's current state, eliminate waste, and redesign a future state. During the redesign, the leaders responsible for the process came together to discuss issues and sign off on what needed to change, as the PIE team needed these leaders' buy-in.

From PIE success emerged an aggressive goal to save one million hours internally by eliminating non-value steps and improving the way the bank operated. A major transformation in people's thinking resulted, and the goal changed from *cutting costs* to *saving hours*. As PIE became increasingly more successful, the goal of saving one million hours internally was redefined to saving 100 million *customer* hours externally. This paralleled the bank's goal of becoming more customer centric. Setting this increased target reflected the success of the PIE approach. By 2014, 250 million customer hours had been eliminated. PIE evolved into customer mapping under the Digital Wave.

Best Practices #4: Triple E Framework

The bank developed a holistic Triple E Framework to create a meaningful learning environment for its people and assist them to progress in their careers. The framework's components included education, experience, and exposure.

- Education – integrated learning experiences including role plays, simulations, mobile and social learning, and hackathons
- Experience – cross-country and cross-functional assignments, international mobility, participation in strategic task forces, and short-term rotations
- Exposure – systematic networking with senior leaders as well as mentoring and coaching

To encourage employee engagement and nurture talent from within, the bank adopted a new internal mobility policy called "2+2" and "3+3":

- 2+2 – AVPs and below could apply for another role within the bank after two years and, if accepted, their supervisors had to release them within two months of acceptance.
- 3+3 – VPs and above could apply for another role within the bank after three years and, if accepted, be released from their current position within three months of acceptance.
- Improving the culture included introducing a "5@5" policy. In Asia, bank employees are notorious for long working hours, so the 5@5 initiative allowed employees to go home at five o'clock on Friday afternoons—a breakthrough.

The goal was to evolve the bank's culture—something that needed to happen from within.

Best Practices #5: HCD

The bank's customer-centric approach, which had taken on an integral role in the bank, was already moving toward customer journeys and innovation through human-centered design (HCD) in 2012. The aim was to create a culture of innovation by teaching people relevant skills so anyone in the bank could innovate.

With these best practices in place through the implementation of the Asia Wave, leaders had unconsciously started to lay the groundwork for the Digital Wave.

CHAPTER 4

The Digital Wave

After the leadership meeting in Phuket in 2014, DBS set about implementing the Digital Wave. Becoming the Asian Bank of Choice for the New Asia had been at the heart of the Asia Wave. As the Digital Wave evolved, at its heart was Making Banking Joyful. The aim was to focus on customer journeys and leverage the opportunities from the plethora of new technologies being launched. The result? To make banking invisible and thus a joyful experience for customers. Every area of the bank started to implement Making Banking Joyful for its customers.

At that time, Piyush's concern was that many organizations tweaked their front-end systems or simply updated their websites rather than transforming from the core. That kind of thinking contributes to why two-thirds of digital implementations fail, according to various research.[5]

"It's not enough to apply digital lipstick." – *Piyush (CEO)*

---

5 Why do most transformations fail? A conversation with Harry Robinson, McKinsey & Co, https://www.mckinsey.com/business-functions/transformation/our-insights/why-do-most-transformations-fail-a-conversation-with-harry-robinson.

Therefore, the leadership team set out to embed the Digital Wave throughout the bank while consistently addressing transformation from the customer's perspective. Piyush was determined to ensure the Digital Wave would not be perceived as an IT initiative, especially as it was *not*.

To transform into a complete digitally driven bank and not just apply digital lipstick, he stated these four priorities:

1. **Creating a positive customer experience through an interface that streamlines the whole journey.** For example, the bank introduced a digital wallet app called DBS PayLah! that allowed people to do banking on their cell phones. It was designed for convenience and security but also social fun. Another example is having digital channels to onboard customers for scale. So, DBS launched Online Account Opening in which SMEs could onboard customers in a simple, fast, and easy process. Also, DBS was the first bank in Asia to digitize its loan application. That began to mean in Singapore's branches, for example, SMEs were now able to apply for up to 11 types of loan products online. It allowed them to track the application online and receive instant notifications on the loan processing. In another example, SME customers in Hong Kong could also apply for loans via a mobile app and receive in-principle approval within an hour.
2. **Digitalizing services through mobile means and analytics while eliminating paper.** To achieve this, the bank used SOA (Service-Oriented Architecture) and an API (Application Program Interface) framework. These digital services eliminated paper and provided

instant fulfillment for customers who realized income and expense benefits from them.

3. **Creating a new business model based on leveraging technology.** This goal required shifting away from revenue earned from fees and margins.
4. **Nurturing a sense of purpose for employees in the work environment.** Doing this acted as a compass for making decisions and creating an empowered, engaged workforce.

These four priorities enabled the bank's leaders to align their thinking and articulate the drive toward transformation.

Communicating Making Banking Joyful Internally

For all employees to be engaged, they had to understand the new strategy being implemented.

The bank created a one-page image that captured the strategy. The image represented a house with "Making Banking Joyful" on the roof and included the five Asian pillars. The foundation of the house included these strategic priorities: embracing the digital world, embedding customer journeys, and living our PRIDE! values. The background was the skyline of Singapore.

Communicating Making Banking Joyful Externally

With the new strategy came a new external branding called "Live More, Bank Less."

When DBS tested the strategy's name, Making Banking Joyful, on customers, they found that customers didn't understand it. The bank then determined to create new external branding.

The external tagline captured what DBS wanted to achieve in the consumer's mind. That is, if the bank conducted financial services in the way customers thought they should, less hassle and tediousness should result. The anxiety customers felt about dealing with a bank then receded while they appreciated having more time to "live life the way they want to live it."

In fact, people liked the idea that DBS was bold enough to say Live More, Bank Less—that banking should be seamlessly part of living life, free of tedious financial transactions. By integrating banking into customers' lives, turning to DBS to achieve financial goals became joyful. Making this happen required DBS to be flexible and nimble while also customer obsessed.

This video from the bank's website further explains the concept of making banking invisible: www.dbs.com/livemore/about-dbs.html.

To implement the strategy, the leadership team crafted three strategic principles to equally embrace. They were:

- Become Digital to the Core
- Embed Ourselves in the Customer Journey
- Culture by Design, and Think Like a Start-up

1. Become Digital to the Core

Making this shift to digital required an expensive investment in DBS's core platform, which took between five and ten years.

The leadership team saw a need to embrace a complete re-architecting of technology. The Asia Wave was considered a "down payment" on the whole digital transformation process.

The team also recognized that becoming digital to the core required rethinking the whole technology architecture and that rethinking the technology architecture required a return to fundamentals: the core platforms, the legacy systems, the networks, and the data centers. Each area needed to be rethought.

The leadership team saw a need to embrace a complete re-architecting of technology.

2. Embed Ourselves in the Customer Journey

This is another way of stating how to be relentlessly customer focused. The real difference started by reimagining the "job to be done" for the customer—a term now embedded in the bank's language to define and frame what needs to be done. This phrase was adopted from Clayton Christensen's work on innovation based on customers' needs.[6]

This is another way of stating how to be relentlessly customer focused.

Specifically, the bank adopted design thinking and trained employees to use an approach called 4Ds: Discover, Define, Develop, and Deliver. The 4Ds approach taught people to adopt customer-journey thinking and reconsider how to define the customer value proposition.

Bank leaders vigorously believed that customer centricity should be the Digital Wave's highest priority. This goal differed from other organizations that put either technology or employee centricity at the top.

---

6 Clayton M. Christensen, et al., "Know Your Customers' 'Jobs to Be Done,'" HBR.org, September 2016, https://hbr.org/2016/09/know-your-customers-jobs-to-be-done.

3. Culture by Design, and Think Like a Start-up

DBS's strategic component of transformation is to continually change its culture. This goal required identifying what aspects of its culture needed to transform as well as how to think and operate like a start-up organization. Leaders wanted the employees to learn new tools, to experiment, fail fast, and fail forward. They were expected to create a minimum viable product (MVP), work in small agile teams, and invariably take more risk..

This goal required identifying what aspects of its culture needed to transform as well as how to think and operate like a start-up organization.

To delve deeper into changing the culture to support the Digital Wave, the bank's leaders studied the practices of leading technology organizations. From their study, they determined they needed to:

- Adopt agile
- Be a learning organization
- Be customer obsessed
- Be data driven
- Encourage risk and experiment

Each of the three strategic principles are explained in depth in the following chapters.

CHAPTER 5

First Strategy Principle of Digital Wave:

Become Digital to the Core

Introduction

DBS has successfully digitized the whole bank to the core. This required creating a rock-solid foundation of core systems the bank could build on and orchestrating a complete transformation of the bank from front to back. The transformation focused on making the bank nimbler and faster in responding to customers.

This required creating a rock-solid foundation of core systems the bank could build on and orchestrating a complete transformation of the bank from front to back.

From the start, the leadership identified that if the bank was going to be digital to the core and act like a technology organization, it was best to learn from the technology greats, figure out how they did it, and identify key aspects the bank could adopt.

To create a rock-solid foundation of core systems to build on, the bank also invested the time and money during the Asia Wave to transform. It did so by putting in place common platforms that were strategic across all of its locations. Then leaders started to identify how to become nimbler, accelerate speed to market, and increase cadence. They designed a new architecture for the bank's technology infrastructure in the back end and focused on being cloud native. That enabled scalability through all the ecosystem partners and improved business/technology while co-working with the maximum use of data.

The technology in the bank transformed from an annoying bottleneck to an acute enabler and driver for the business.

We Are a Tech Company

DBS employees were naturally ingrained to think as bankers. But for the bank to successfully embrace the Digital Wave, leaders recognized it needed employees to stop thinking they worked in a bank. Instead, they had to start thinking they worked in a tech company.

But for the bank to successfully embrace the Digital Wave, leaders recognized it needed employees to stop thinking they worked in a bank. Instead, they had to start thinking they worked in a tech company.

Today, it is not unusual to hear different organizations using the expression, "We are a tech company." In 2015, however, DBS was one of the first organizations to adopt this approach. The essential question became how to change the mindset of employees.

> "At DBS, we act less like a bank and more like a tech company."
> – *Piyush (CEO)*[7]

What Would Jeff Do?

To change the way the bank framed the digital transformation and to think like a tech company, the bank considered how Amazon CEO Jeff Bezos ran his company. This knowledge then led to adopting the question across the bank, "What would Jeff do?" It meant employees would shift from thinking like bankers—thus turning to banking approaches as solutions—to thinking like a tech company that creates digital-driven solutions, as Amazon does.

The question "What would Jeff do?" caught on. Asking it helped elevate the thought processes and approach employees needed as they adopted a digital mindset at DBS.

A catchphrase alone, however, was not enough. To support employees in adopting digitally driven solutions, the technology across the bank needed to create a rock-solid foundation of core systems.

GANDALF

After visiting different tech companies in the West, the bank came up with an acronym that captured the technology

7 Breana Patel, "'At DBS, we act less like a bank and more like a tech company.' With DBS Bank CEO Piyush Gupta," DBS.com, October 12, 2018, www.dbs.com/innovation/dbs-innovates/at-dbs-we-act-less-like-a-bank-and-more-like-a-tech-company-with-dbs-bank-ceo-piyush-gupta.html.

transformation—GANDALF. GANDALF is the wizard in *The Hobbit* and *The Lord of the Rings* novels by J. R. R. Tolkien.

In this acronym, G is for Google—using open-source software like Google. A is for Amazon—running on Amazon's cloud platforms. N is for Netflix—using data and automation to scale and provide personalized recommendations as Netflix does. A is for Apple—designing systems as Apple does. L is for LinkedIn—pushing for continuous learning, and F is for Facebook—becoming more community focused.

What about the **D**? The bank, DBS, would be the D in GANDALF—the digital and data bank of Singapore.

GANDALF resulted in comparing the bank's digital transformation to the best technology organizations, not to other banks. This is an important distinction. To become the world's best bank, you can't copy other banks. You have to think more like a tech organization than a bank.

GANDALF resulted in comparing the bank's digital transformation to the best technology organizations, not to other banks. This is an important distinction.

Before long, a sense of urgency emerged as people started working faster and reframing the customer perspective. GANDALF acted like a lightning rod to spark all employees to think like a tech organization.

Employees resonated with being set free in their thinking, which showed up in several ways. A prime example was the creation of a group of GANDALF scholars to support employee development. Each of them was given $1,000 and told to go learn something meaningful. When they came back from their classes, they had to teach others what they had learned. Knowing they had to teach others ensured that they listened well in their trainings. This approach reached more than 15,000 employees!

Five Key Technology Initiatives

GANDALF provided a new mindset and acted as a lightning rod as the Technology and Operations (T&O) team turned to building the digital architecture. It first identified these five key technology initiatives from the GANDALF organizations that the bank needed to adopt:

1. **Shift from products to platform** – To move from long-term projects over three to five years with steering committees and bureaucracy to teams having a "control to context" approach. The business owns the platforms; technology provides the impetus and funding.
2. **Develop high-performing agile teams** – To be agile and eliminate long-term projects and their shackles, then reorganize to put both tech and business teams on level terms by having *shared* goals instead of different goals. The shared goals also have shared measures.
3. **Automate everything** – To allow faster building, testing, and deploying of systems. The focus turned to increasing cadence so systems releases could occur faster than before.
4. **Design for modern systems** – To engineer technologies and build systems that are scalable, elastic, and ready for experimentation. Driving this strategy required using the cloud.
5. **Organize for success** – To provide employees with the right tools and support to drive an agile way of working.

By 2018, the GANDALF transformation targets had evolved into these three:

1. Become "cloud native" – reducing costs and improving resilience and scalability
2. Increase Release Cadence 10X – reducing time to market or speed of work
3. Build for APIs and Performance – becoming even more customer centric and extending GANDALF to ecosystems

1. Become "Cloud Native"

For organizations, simply moving a little toward "cloud native" can provide about a 20 percent savings. For DBS, it was not a case of "lift and shift"—that is, taking hardware and moving it to the cloud but using the same people and software. This approach could be distracting, and it would not generate the desired savings and effectiveness. Bank leaders did not want "cloud lipstick"; they wanted "cloud to the core."

The bank's cloud native strategy focused on three components: hardware, software, and people.

- Hardware – sharing up capacity
- Software – using open source to reduce costs and leverage the customization to automate
- People – adopting agile and DevOps (allowing for better understanding between engineers and the business, resulting in greater accountability overall)

As the bank grew, the technology demand increased. But at the same time, the T&O team:

- Reduced the group infrastructure costs by around $50 million
- Reduced its server footprint by 80 percent, including the number of physical machines, while doing five times the volume it had been doing
- Made a staggering 75 percent reduction in data center space usage by 2019

While some banks are consolidating data centers and moving partly to the cloud, DBS consolidated the physical data centers a few years ago. Its current data centers are a quarter of the size they were in 2015, yet they can generate 10 times more capacity to scale up when required.

Adopting cloud technology has allowed DBS to share capacity, use resources equally across different businesses, automate, reduce costs, and respond faster to its various businesses. For example, a business can ask to double its capacity requirements without warning the T&O team, and team members are able to comply. Previously, they required weeks of notice.

A key factor in adopting cloud for DBS was not whether it was a private or public cloud but its usability and fit for the bank's growth. Ensuring solid security had to be an underlying principle. The advantage of adopting a public cloud is being able to rev up capacity by simply paying for more of it as you need it. It was apparent the bank could focus its systems' efficiency better using a private cloud than a public cloud.

As a result, technology transformed from a bottleneck to an enabler and driver for the bank's business.

Today, more than 99 percent of the bank's open systems are cloud enabled with over 60 applications being completely cloud native. As a result, technology transformed from a bottleneck to an enabler and driver for the bank's business. For example, through Continuous Integration and Continuous Delivery, the bank is able to deliver 300,000 automated builds and 30,000 code releases monthly—an increase of almost 10 times compared with previous performance.

2. Increase Release Cadence 10X

"What would Jeff do?" This question challenged the bank to think like a tech company. In the traditional approach of gathering requirements followed by developing and testing and then the release, only some learning occurred. The real learning came from getting a product to market fast, as Amazon does, and then testing and learning. This meant restructuring not only the approach but the culture, organization, and cadence so the bank could respond to its customers quickly and keep improving its products. Improving cadence allowed the bank to move faster.

Establishing a faster cadence also required the automation of all applications as well as automated testing. Aggressive automation enabled the bank to move faster and increase its efficiency. This is important because when an organization moves faster, it is susceptible to making more mistakes. That means it must be quicker at evaluating and responding. So, for example, when the bank fully automated the deployment of its applications, its automatic testing increased 10 times.

Through automation, the bank's cadence improved dramatically—by 8.5 times. As an added benefit, DBS's fast cadence demonstrated to external partners how quick and responsive the bank had become.

As technology needs expanded in 2015, data warehousing became a critical part of an organization's digital transformation. The standard approach—building to demand and being specific to requirement—could take up to two years. But that standard was too slow for DBS's technology appetite!

The T&O team initially redesigned the technology to reduce the timeline of infrastructure projects from two years to less than six months. This involved developing the business initiative, analyzing the component requirements, identifying action steps, and sourcing funding. Using the standard approach, all that could take six months—and that's before ever starting project implementation. The team automated the whole up-front process.

Standardization and digitalization of the infrastructure allowed for easier scaling to the bank's requirements. It also made experimenting easier and supported the development of agile across the business. This was possible because the technology changes were made to respond quickly to the bank's business requirements.

As T&O continues to strive to improve the release cadence, today the timeline of infrastructure projects is less than one day!

3. Build for APIs and Performance

As early as 2011, the T&O team was studying the potential of APIs (Application Programming Interfaces or micro-services as they'd been called) but first had to explain to bankers what APIs were. The team used an image of a mobile phone connected to a computer to show the connection between two systems.

In 2017, DBS successfully launched the world's largest banking API platform with more than 150 live APIs. Today, it has more than 1,000 APIs and over 400 partners plugged into its API platform.

Developing an API platform led to DBS's ability to leverage start-ups and attract partners by being an ecosystem player. More than that, it has earned a reputation of being easy to work with while its performance keeps improving.

CHAPTER 6

Changing Technology's DNA

The T&O team ensured that the bank's technology would be at the forefront to support its growing business in new, resilient ways. This involved changing the bank's technology DNA by initially identifying innovative ways to scale cloud-based technologies, apply modern frameworks, deploy automation best practices, and dramatically improve speed to market. (Speed to market is measured from the time an idea is first developed until the technology is in the hands of customers and employees.)

Various techniques were integrated by the T&O team to support the seismic shift of the technology DNA.

1. Design for No Ops – DFNO

DFNO proved to be an important early success and key turning point in understanding what digital transformation meant to operations. It was also the catalyst for digitalizing operations in other parts of the bank and included revisiting legacy operations. The idea was to measure anything that moved. The team didn't always know how to do it, but the challenge to accomplish the goal had begun.

Design for No Ops (DFNO) is not about completely redesigning what goes on with *no* operations involved. Rather, it is about eliminating unnecessary components and focusing on the value add—delighting customers. The concept articulates an imaginary state or outcome. Thus, DFNO is a process that defines an outcome requiring instant gratification without "Failure Demand" (any job that arises because it wasn't done properly the first time) and with no follow-up needed to produce a differentiated customer experience. To ensure customers are being delighted, the bank uses data instrumentation to measure, monitor, and control processes by providing real-time knowledge of customers' journeys.

DFNO proved to be an important early success and key turning point in understanding what digital transformation meant to operations.

2. From Failure Demand to Demand Management

The bank focused on creating a language that brought the culture of operations and business together. From this, the term "Failure Demand" evolved into "Demand Management." This addressed the chasm of a business focused on revenue without caring about the challenges this focus caused in operations. Designing for "No Ops" became part of Demand Management.

Demand Management is the practice of identifying and measuring all work done across the entire value chain (demand) and systematically working to eliminate, migrate, and optimize this work for higher productivity, lower cost, and improved customer satisfaction (management). It also aims to reduce Failure Demand by leveraging customer journeys or using analytics or designing better products or migrating customers to digital transactions.

In the span of three years (from 2014 to 2017), DBS released 100 percent of its automated applications, while the volume of automated test executions increased tenfold. This aggressive automation resulted in reduced time to market.

3. Adopt "Toil" Approach from Google

"Toil" is a term DBS adopted from Google, referring to the kind of work tied to running a production service that tends to be manual, repetitive, automatable, tactical, devoid of enduring value, and scaled linearly as a service grows.[8]

In 2016, the bank turned its focus to removing toil from the technology operations and segregating the head count required to *operate* from the head count required to *build* new architecture. This allowed clarity of work that drove how toil would operate. It also provided an ability to optimize that work while reducing the toil.

Typically, there is more toil in legacy applications than cloud native. Therefore, the drive toward cloud native applications not only led to faster development but also made applications more flexible. In this way, the entire "operate" effort was reduced. DFNO served to remove manual toil from the system.

Today, having less toil in cloud native allows for greater speed and agility across the organization and higher efficiency in its operations. The collaboration, end-to-end thinking, and customer obsession across the organization created opportunities to remove toil and make changes that ultimately improved the customer experience. Internally, the right changes allowed teams to focus on value-adding work, which improved employee engagement and built excitement for implementing the Digital Wave.

---

8 Vivek Raul, "Chapter 5: Eliminating Toil," SRE (Sebastopol, CA: O'Reilly Media, 2017), https://landing.google.com/sre/sre-book/chapters/eliminating-toil/.https://landing.google.com/sre/sre-book/chapters/eliminating-toil/.

4. Application Errors

Previously in the IT industry, the more changes made to an application, the more vulnerable it was to errors. The view was that fewer changes resulted in stability and better performance. In agile organizations, though, the rate of making changes in applications is considerably higher than before, yet their rate of error is lower! Why?

When an organization has been built using the agile approach—automating and testing all deployments and then making numerous changes within a day—the errors are typically small and contained. Also, the error rate and its resulting impact is low because the errors apply only across a small service.

5. Outsourcing to Insourcing

In 2009, 85 percent of the bank's technology work was being outsourced. The bank's T&O employees at the time were mainly signing contracts and managing vendors. In effect, they were in the contract management business, not the technology business. Over the next few years, the bank set out to reverse this ratio. By 2018, T&O was 90 percent self-managed, and many of the required skills were present internally, not externally. With this technology DNA, the bank could design, build, and operate its own technology with a team of about 6,000 people.

The next chapter shares the best practices that successfully resulted in the bank becoming digital to the core.

CHAPTER 7

Best Practices for Becoming Digital to the Core

To support the transformation of becoming digital to the core, DBS adopted various initiatives. The leaders knew where they wanted the organization to go and what they had to do; they just wanted to get on with it. As a result, the following best practices evolved.

Best Practices Adopted for Digital

Best Practice #1: Two-in-a-Box

"Business is technology and technology is business" is the aggressive rally call that reverberated across the whole bank. It could have just sounded like a slogan, but it had the structure and rituals to support it. The two-in-a-box structure supporting the bank's transformation was tremendously successful.

The term "two-in-a-box" describes how the tech and business heads collaborated to understand each other's business through shared objectives and measures. Specifically, each business head learned the others' responsibilities, thus allowing them to switch roles. Even when presenting to the CEO, the tech and business heads needed to be able to represent each other's job.

To achieve this collaboration, the heads genuinely needed to share the same goals, measures, and understanding of the challenges. They also needed a common understanding of what had to be done, not just pay lip service to each other's business requirements.

The term "two-in-a-box" describes how the tech and business heads collaborated to understand each other's business through shared objectives and measures.

This two-in-a-box best practice successfully established the platform for each business to become more knowledgeable about the technology required and vice versa. It continues to play an important role in the way the bank operates.

Best Practice #2: Reverse Mentors

The business leaders were assigned a reverse mentor from technology and other departments. Having a reverse mentor gave them opportunities to learn areas of the business through one-on-one meetings. It also allowed them to ask questions they might not feel comfortable asking while in meetings or in situations where they were expected to know all the answers.

Having a reverse mentor gave them opportunities to learn areas of the business through one-on-one meetings.

The business leaders leveraged this initiative by, for example, learning the differences between Java, HTML, and Python. Other examples were learning about cloud infrastructure and machine learning.

Feeling psychologically safe is critical in any transformation. The reverse mentoring initiative created a safe environment in which leaders could ask questions they normally wouldn't dare to ask or, as we say in Asia, be seen "losing face." An added benefit was that the reverse mentor learned what the leaders were doing.

Best Practice #3: Establishing a Culture of Experimentation

As the bank set about understanding and improving what its customers wanted, it required a culture of innovation driven partly by a new openness to experiment. Rather than a focus on creating products, people experimented with various options so they could identify the best solutions for their customers.

The team started by democratizing training and providing employees with a central framework to help them drive their own journeys and experiments.

The bank's transformation team focused on building an innovation mentality by engaging everyone as part of the digital transformation. The team started by democratizing training and providing employees with a central framework to help them drive their own journeys and experiments.

In addition, it fostered partnerships with the Fintech start-up community and developed a network among start-up communities. For example, the team collaborated with more than 15,000 employees using different experimental formats such as hackathons, accelerator programs, and Xchange programs.

Best Practice #4: DBS Xchange Program

This business-matching program connected DBS Bank and its enterprise clients with start-ups to co-create tech solutions that solved business pain points. Through Fintech partnerships, the bank aimed to develop a robust Fintech ecosystem that was boosted by innovation. They transformed people's experiences with financial services while creating a more accessible market for start-ups and innovative entrepreneurs.

Launched in Singapore and Hong Kong in 2018, Start-Up Xchange continues to help both start-ups and DBS project partners achieve shared business goals through design thinking and experimentation. With four out of five accelerators typically failing (according to the bank's own research), Startup Xchange addresses the challenges to ensure sustained support from the collaborators in the program.

As part of the bank's five-year $10 million investment made in 2015, the program continues to support the growth of Fintech start-ups through four key areas of technology: artificial intelligence, data science, immersive media, and the Internet of Things. By harnessing the power of these emerging technologies, DBS and its clients can fulfill their customers' business and lifestyle needs more quickly and seamlessly than ever before.

To date, Start-Up Xchange has introduced hundreds of start-ups to units within the bank as well as to the bank's SME customers to solve their pain points. This system has resulted in successfully rolling out numerous emerging technology solutions.

In addition to helping the bank and its customers digitize their businesses, Start-Up Xchange allows start-ups to showcase the solutions they developed for the bank. When they're raising capital with the investor community, they can name DBS Bank as an anchor client—a big advantage.

One example of a successful Start-Up Xchange project was "impress.ai." This Singapore-based start-up (and SME customer for DBS) partnered with DBS's HR team to create JIM, Southeast Asia's first virtual bank recruiter. (JIM is explained in detail later in this book.)

By 2017, the bank stopped trying to count the number of experiments going on; doing so became too cumbersome. It had been tracking numbers not because they were important in themselves but to catalyze different experiments. Once the program was embedded into the bank's culture, there was no need to continue the count.

Best Practice #5: New Technology for Older Employees

A few years ago, Piyush was back in New Delhi visiting his 85-year-old father. During the visit, his father did his banking online, paid his taxes online, and bought something for his mother on Amazon. Piyush reasoned that if his 85-year-old father could make this digital change in his personal life, why couldn't people in their 30s, 40s, 50s, and 60s change in their professional lives?

He realized that the *person* as much as the *environment* fosters change. With that in mind, Piyush returned from India, driven to let his employees learn by doing and to create an environment in which they had permission to take risks.

Many organizations tend to look at young people to adopt new technology and keep their older employees working with technology that's dying out. Piyush wanted everybody to work on both the old and the new technologies. He gave older employees an opportunity to work on the new technology *if* they could qualify. Within a year, after each one was given $1,000 to choose courses they wanted to participate in, 90 percent qualified. (Of the $1,000, $500 came from DBS and $500 came from the Singapore government's program sponsoring the nation to upskill itself.)

DBS employees of all ages rose to the challenge, affirming that people can change when given the ability and aspiration to do so.

DBS employees of all ages rose to the challenge, affirming that people can change when given the ability and aspiration to do so.

Piyush was also influenced by meeting with Peter Ma, chairman and founder of Ping An Insurance Group. Ma explained that older employees were like sheep and newer employees were like wolves. This statement had a profound impact on Piyush.

> "I'm going to make my sheep, wolves. When 70-year-old people are using smartphones, the notion that you can't change in work is inconceivable to me." – *Piyush (CEO)*[9]

Best Practice #6: Digital Is Everyone's Responsibility

The T&O leadership team had a clear answer—"No"—to this question: Do we have a separate team to drive the new technology requirements? The leaders envisioned everyone across the bank feeling part of the business responsibility and transformation. They wanted employees to believe digital transformation was their responsibility, not the tech team's responsibility alone.

Best Practice #7: Hack to Hire Program

"Hack to Hire" became a creative way for the bank to identify and hire the right people as developers, data scientists, scrum

9 "Euromoney: How Gupta turned DBS into the bank of the future," DBS.com, accessed April 19, 2021, https://www.dbs.com/about-us/who-we-are/awards-accolades/a-world-first/euromoney-awards-for-excellence.

masters, system engineers, and other talent. Rather than conducting traditional interviews, the bank created a Hack to Hire Program to find the best of the best people to employ.

This initiative involved sending out some coding and technical changes on a website. The top 200 performers who responded were then invited into DBS over a weekend where they performed some hacking and took on other challenges. The focus was not on what they hacked and came up with but on whether they had the right skill set and how they worked as a team in an agile environment. The prize for the best of the best at the end of the two days was being offered a job before that person left the building. It was no longer necessary to say, "We will get back to you."

The first time DBS ran this Hack to Hire Program in India, 12,000 people signed up. Over the years, the bank has received over 100,000 applicants from these programs and hired hundreds of people. Its original hires are now running the Hack to Hire Program.

A sobering thought is that today, DBS has over 6,600 software engineers in the organization, which means it has more engineers than bankers! Now that's digital to the core.

Questions for Consideration

1. Where does digitalization add value to your business?
2. If you built your business from scratch today, what would you change?
3. What is your digital purpose?
4. What measures track your digitalization efforts?
5. How does technology provide an opportunity to redesign your business model?
6. What is your architecture technology plan?
7. What is your budget for transforming your technology architecture?
8. Which technologies are your customers predominantly using?
9. Which technologies could best improve your customers' experience?
10. Which technologies could best improve your efficiency and control costs?
11. What are your cloud-computing opportunities?
12. Have can you speed up your technology cadence?
13. How can you leverage DevOps?
14. How can you adopt agile?
15. How can you build dynamic scalability?

16. How can you design for no-ops?
17. How can you design for AI-ops?
18. Where can you leverage machine learning?
19. How can you shift from project to platforms?
20. Where do you need to build APIs?
21. How can you remove toil in the process?
22. How can your organization become paperless?
23. What training do your employees need to create higher-performing teams?

CHAPTER 8

Second Strategy Principle of Digital Wave:

Embed Ourselves in the Customer Journey

Introduction

DBS focused on embedding itself in the customer's journey. The goal was no longer about the product or service but about being customer obsessed—to make banking invisible by leveraging technology and adopting customer journey thinking throughout the organization. This approach drove every employee toward becoming customer obsessed.

The bank took the perspective that customers didn't wake up in the morning wanting to do banking; they woke up wanting to buy a car or a house or an investment. Banking provided the means to an end, while technology provided the means for the bank to make many steps of the customer journey invisible.

DBS leaders became even more customer obsessed by constantly asking, "Is this change making banking joyful for our customers?" From that core question, they adopted design thinking and solutions based on their *customers'* perspective.

Design Thinking, called "4Ds" in DBS's terminology, guided employees to know what needed to be done. The bank designed solutions that improved the "jobs to be done." The *overall* job to be done in the Digital Wave was Making Banking Joyful, which involved stepping back from the day-to-day business to identify the customer journey and continuously improve upon it.

A prime example was that the bank didn't focus on selling more mortgages; it focused instead on the "job to be done" for the customer, which was helping individuals realize their dreams. Adopting a customer journey approach for mortgages started with customer communication as many as six months ahead of time. The goal was for the bank to be part of the complete home-buying experience. The bank representative assisted in looking for the right home, comparing options, and supporting the process of identifying the best mortgage for a customer.

Today, the bank continues to enhance customer journeys by developing APIs as part of its ecosystem strategy while continuing to collaborate with ecosystem partners.

The chapters that follow explain how the bank embedded itself in its customer journeys by becoming customer obsessed.

CHAPTER 9

Putting Our Customer at the Heart of Everything We Do

Some organizations' approach to solving a customer problem has been to form a team, brainstorm what's required, and then create a solution based on its assumptions of what customers want. Thus, the team determines what's best for the customer.

As DBS became more customer obsessed, it looked for ways to ensure innovations and digitalization were truly customer driven. This required having an innovation and design topology approach, so the bank adopted the 4Ds approach from the UK Design Council.[10]

Design Thinking: 4Ds Framework

The 4Ds framework became the methodology used to conduct customer journeys across the bank. The term "4D" stands for:

10 "What is the framework for innovation? Design Council's evolved Double Diamond," Design Council.org, accessed April 13, 2021, https://www.designcouncil.org.uk/news-opinion/what-framework-innovation-design-councils-evolved-double-diamond.

- Discover – gathering and synthesizing insights and inspirations from customers
- Define – refining opportunities and concepts
- Develop – testing the riskiest assumptions, then aligning and planning the implementation
- Deliver – implementing the concept

Discover, the first step in the journey, required the most time—as much as 50 percent. Many people wanted to jump straight to Deliver, but they had to be pulled back.

Become Customer Obsessed, Not Internally Obsessed

Implementing 4Ds involved each employee focusing on customer immersion and becoming more engaged with other departments and stakeholders in the customers' journeys. The resulting collaboration broke down traditional silos and enabled employees to become customer obsessed rather than internally obsessed.

The resulting collaboration broke down traditional silos and enabled employees to become customer obsessed rather than internally obsessed.

Cross-Sell to Cross-Buy

With increased data available, the bank started using contextual online marketing that adopted targeted advertising based on user behavior and information.

This shift to contextual marketing led to a mindset change from "cross-sell" to "cross-buy." Cross-sell happens when you purchase a product from the bank and another product is offered to you. For example, when you open a bank account, you are asked if you would like a credit card.

The mindset shift came from the GANDALF learning—that was, instead of a single product being pushed on a customer, a suite of options are offered. The system is similar to when you buy a book online and five other books are recommended. This contextual marketing outcome reveals what appeals to a particular customer at a certain point in time.

This shift to contextual marketing led to a mindset change from "cross-sell" to "cross-buy."

From analyzing customer data in cross-buying, the bank learned that the more customers became engaged with its offerings, the more business they did with the bank.

Building Prototypes, Not Slide Deck Presentations

A key advantage of adopting design thinking was the speed the organization could create prototype solutions for its customers. Instead of employees having to build slide deck presentations, propose solutions to leaders, and ask for their approval and resources, teams were empowered to build prototypes for customer approval.

Design Thinking in Action

The Global Transaction Services (GTS) team emphasized that one of the critical "jobs to be done" for their customers was assisting CFOs and corporate treasurers to simulate various bank and corporate solutions at no cost. Doing so would identify potential opportunities that could maximize value for their enterprise. At the time, the process had many pain points, so the time was ripe for a customer journey to adopt the 4Ds framework.

> "If there's one bank shaking up cash management globally, it's Asian bank DBS." – *Euromoney*[11]

The following example demonstrates how 4D was adopted within DBS.

DBS Treasury Prism

CFOs and corporate treasurers had to typically manage several accounts with various currencies and transaction flows across numerous countries. This process involved having a relationship with different banks in order to optimize their treasury and cash management solutions. CFOs and/or corporate treasurers were also challenged in keeping pace with regulatory changes in the different markets they traded. The whole process involving multiple parties was laborious and time-consuming.

In 2017, DBS launched Treasury Prism, one of the world's first online treasury and cash management simulation tools. This tool has allowed customers to:

11 Clive Horwood, "The Cash Management Conundrum," Euromoney.com, October 2018, https://www.dbs.com.sg/iwov-resources/forms/euromoney/en/advisory/euromoney-cash-management-conundrum-2018.pdf.

- Model their cash management structures easily and at no cost.
- Identify an optimal solution by choosing from the full range of potential solutions that best fit their business objectives.
- Analyze the benefits and cost implications of the chosen structure to support their business case.

A 20-person team from various departments set about developing a collaboration platform. The team used algorithms that could produce an optimal outcome based on yield, costs, and risk mitigation. The algorithms could also produce a variety of options so if the first didn't work, the second approach could be set in motion.

DBS Treasury Prism has received five global and regional innovation awards and has quickly gained a core community of corporate treasury users. These have led to more than 3,000 optimal cash management structures and solutions, many of them with DBS.

A project of this scope—with so many different functions and parties involved—would typically take years to complete. But the team wanted to build the new solution in months. This ambitious and aggressive goal was made possible as the culture of the bank, the technology architecture, and its core way of operating was transforming. For example, the team used an agile approach, so instead of the development team spending time traveling to the head office to give progress updates, senior leaders traveled or video-conferenced into the co-located business and technology squad. Instead of a slide deck presentation, management received stand-up updates—to keep them short—of the developing solution.

Embracing cloud-based architecture allowed the team to leapfrog the competition by being agile and structuring the business without cost. At that time, bank legacy systems had become an anchor that was drastically slowing down processes, increasing the cost of becoming a digital-centric business and offering customers slower service and more expensive products.

The group strategy aligned perfectly with GTS needs. Becoming business agile, which was rapidly being adopted across the bank, was the solution. Everyone involved worked to develop a minimal viable product (MVP) for delivery within months instead of years.

Discover – Gathering and Synthesizing Insights and Inspirations

The bank formed a cross-functional team in which all team members had a vested interest in the area to be improved. The guideline for the size of the team was the "two-pizza rule"—that is, only enough people to consume two pizzas! If more people were on the team, then agile methodology tended to struggle.

At DBS, the Discovery step started by envisioning the "job to be done" from the customer's perspective. This became the journey statement, which stated the value the task or job would add both to customers and to the bank. Any solution had to benefit everyone.

The journey statement identified and directed the team through Discovery and was present throughout all four stages. An example journey statement is: "We want to enable treasury and finance professionals to optimize cash management in a way that is intuitive, interactive, insightful, and trustworthy and to ultimately achieve increased customer advocacy and business."

With this statement in place, the team then conducted a stakeholder mapping of the customer by asking, "Who is involved, and who will benefit from cash management optimization?" The key personas and stakeholders were literally drawn onto a map that showed everyone involved and how they were connected.

The stakeholder map reflected the key roles and connectivity between them that allowed a research plan to be drafted. That plan covered who would be interviewed and how many interviews would be conducted. Discussion guides were then drafted that featured questions the team needed to ask of each stakeholder to ensure consistency and to address the journey statement.

The questions asked were a mix of three elements:

- the functional "job to be done," including roles and responsibilities and KPIs
- the social "job to be done" involving interactivity among stakeholders and how they wanted to be perceived
- the emotional "job to be done" involving how the stakeholders felt in executing the functional job.

Then—and only then—did the team begin customer interviews.

For optimizing cash management, the six members of the part-time cross-functional team spoke to more than 70 corporate treasurers, tax managers, and CFOs over five weeks. Their feedback was captured word for word (not paraphrased) so the emotional "job to be done" was heard by the rest of the team in the targeted customers' language. This helped define and develop solutions that directly addressed the pain points.

For example, in cash management, the team identified one customer's pain point to be the extra time the treasurer spent reviewing a business case for the changes involved in a cash management RFP (Request For Proposal). The aim then became to automate the RFP process to meet the emotional "job to be done" of going home earlier each day during the RFP review. The solution had to directly appeal to customers' specific pain points.

One customer mentioned going to seven different banks seeking to optimize his cash management. He received seven different answers and didn't know which bank to trust. None of these banks was transparent about how it calculated the benefits—and many hadn't even calculated benefits!

After completing customer interviews, the team synthesized the feedback and buried itself in the raw data, identifying and transposing clues onto Post-It notes for affinity clustering. The clues were consolidated into five to ten insights that summarized key findings from the research. As a critical part of the 4Ds methodology, these insights provided the core from which the team could create solutions.

In the cash management example, a number of insights emerged—some expected and others not. One expected insight was that treasurers had little or no time to keep up with the latest regulatory and tax changes, let alone analyze their effects on cash management operations. An unexpected insight was treasurers believing the benefits from an optimal cash management solution were challenging to quantify. They found it even more difficult to find a case for making a change.

Generating insights is a critical stage of the Discovery process. In the 4Ds methodology, this phase should be at least 50 percent of the Discovery, Define, and Development stages. For the cash management team, the Discovery step took six weeks, with the team working part time.

Define – Refining the Opportunities and Concepts

Armed with insights, the team then brainstormed digital approaches to help treasury and finance professionals optimize their cash management. Team members realized they needed to unlearn some concepts, imagine the best possible unconstrained solutions, and then build on them to allow the best ideas to emerge. Using tools such as statement starters, concept posters, lightning critiques, and crowdsourcing ideas, the team asked, "How can we make things easier and better?"

From there, team members started to define the solution as an online simulation and solutioning tool. This tool would allow treasurers to mix and match cash management solutions and products. With it, they could dynamically assess the relative benefits of the solutions versus the impacts of the regulatory and tax environment. With the team working part time, this Define stage took two weeks.

The team continued to refine the best ideas, processes, workflow, and solutions. As part of this stage, it assessed whether the concept would be technically feasible as well as viable—two factors that moved the task from Define to Develop. For example, a solution could well be technically *feasible* but not *viable* if it would cost too much to realize the return expected.

Develop – Testing Your Riskiest Assumptions and Planning the Implementation

In this stage, the team focused on assessing the desirability of the solution. The first prototype for the tool was then developed and tested for the first time with customers against some set hypotheses. Testing came in a variety of means—from physical mock-ups to low-resolution prototypes. The key was to quickly build a tool, share ideas, and document feedback. Also important was testing the most critical and uncertain assumptions about the concept.

In this example, the team created a wireframe prototype in which treasurers could enter financial data and the system would auto-calculate the optimal cash management structure based on yield, cost, and risk. It could also calculate a variety of less optimal structures selected according to the treasurer's preference. This solution spoke directly to earlier insights on the difficulty of quantifying the benefits of relative structures.

The prototype also showed how the tool would check the solution against the regulatory and tax environment across each country. It would advise what could and couldn't be done, which responded directly to another key insight. If the structure was allowed but still required regulatory approval, then the tool would advise what needed to be done.

This solution was tested with 25 customers over a six-week period. The team sat with them to test the prototype while watching their behavior and reactions. The tool was also tested against the journey statement to make sure it was intuitive, interactive, and insightful.

In testing customers, the team captured both their reactions and emotions to understand clearly what they liked and did not like. Then team members redesigned the prototype in response to these reactions and emotions.

In the Develop stage, the team tested different hypotheses and constantly learned from them. On occasion, though, the team was forced to take a leap of faith because not all the required information was available. The final prototype was then reviewed using technology to ensure the tool remained feasible. Once its desirability was confirmed, the team assessed its viability and investment level.

Deliver – Implementing the Concept

The solution was built in the Deliver stage.

More and more, agile practices are adopted in the Deliver stage to create the MVP. At this stage, a cross-functional, co-located, self-governing squad is typically formed. The team involves key members of those who worked in the Discover, Define, and Deliver stages. Coders sit beside the people from the business, while stand-ups (meetings) are used for updates and discussion. Every two weeks, sprint updates are made to foster constant review of customer feedback during the MVP development.

Overall, the Deliver stage requires focusing on a maintained and prioritized program of work, regular demonstration of value, incremental delivery of solution, and a collaborative and empowered team. The MVP is open to anyone, including customers who test it and provide feedback.

In the cash management example, what was the final delivery? DBS's Treasury Prism. (You can find the world's first online treasury and cash management simulation platform at www.treasuryprism.dbs.com.)

Becoming *Euromoney*'s best digital bank in 2016 and 2018 attracted large corporate treasury functions to DBS whose current banks could not fulfill their demands or advance at the pace DBS was already moving.

CHAPTER 10

Customer Journey Examples

This chapter shares both external and internal customer examples of how DBS became totally customer obsessed. The first example was a critical early success, as it demonstrated what could be achieved in the Digital Wave. It describes the creation of a bank in India without any physical presence—Digibank.

External Customer Examples

1. Digibank India

Digibank's launch in India in 2015 aided in changing people's mindset within the bank about what was digitally possible, and it created a cultural shift toward believing in how the bank could leverage digitalization for its customers. Any successful transformation requires early success to build traction and momentum within the organization. For DBS, Digibank represented its initial success.

Digibank demonstrated what the bank could achieve. It changed employee mindsets, created digitalization success stories, and expanded the bank's capabilities. Specifically, it addressed how the bank could obtain customers at scale with no physical presence. In its first year, Digibank acquired two million new customers.

- **Genesis of Digibank**

In 2013, the bank's senior leaders started to strategize about growing organically as opposed to inorganically. This fueled their discussion for building a presence in a country that didn't have a branch footprint.

Around the same time, the bank's customer research revealed that customers were focused on their livelihoods, their families, their interests, and their lives. To them, banking was a means to the end, but still, money was central in their lives. This marked the first morphing of the current strategy. These four words from the interviews started to encapsulate what customers wanted: Bank Less, Live More. The phrase began as a strategy and later evolved into the bank's marketing message.

As part of implementing the Digital Wave, a digital team that formed in 2015 initiated the bank's first hackathon. Using ideas from customers, selected employees worked with external developers in a high-intensity environment supported by a range of tools and resources. The winning idea of that first hackathon was to open an account as quickly as it took to download and install an app. This idea rapidly evolved into the start of a digital banking concept in India that became Digibank.

- **New Technology, New Approach, New Mindset**

In developing the technology to support the new digital approach, the team experimented by testing and learning. Prior to launching the Digital Wave, experimentation in the bank had been limited and controlled. The new strategy encouraged and rewarded people for testing options and taking risks.

As a result of the new culture of experimentation, Digibank became a completely untested mobile bank approach in a country where DBS had never before realized scale.

The three strategic principles of 1) transforming from the core, 2) customer obsession, and 3) culture by design became the ethos for Digibank. The aim was for the digital team to be turbocharged like a start-up. This would be tough if team members also had to manage their regular jobs, so the bank created a separate team that could be nimble and fast.

The aim in building Digibank from the customers' perspective included these elements:

- Customers could open an account in 90 seconds on their smart phones.
- They could open a full bank account without having to go to a physical branch.
- They thought this way of banking and its branding was "cool."

The team adopted an agile approach for the implementation. Before long, they launched and tested various MVPs. The speed at which they responded to customers' feedback had to be fast to not lose them. This resulted in the team pushing out weekly releases and developing a cadence to respond daily to customer feedback.

One of the other early key decisions was that employees would not be running the processes; technology would. This created the goal of designing a bank with 90 percent fewer people than normal, with call centers but without branches. Also, Indian consumers tend to use checks heavily, but the team decided *not* to allow checks, which are physical, not digital. Therefore, anyone wanting to use checks was not the right customer for Digibank.

The team operated with a clean sheet for what it wanted and needed to do to succeed. This removed boundaries and allowed radical, innovative thinking, which came in useful to overcome unanticipated challenges.

- **Digital Know Your Customer (KYC)**

To launch the digital bank, the team had to overcome a number of challenges, such as adopting new technologies, overcoming legal issues, and reaching out to customers.

In India, regulations stated that the customer had to physically show identification to open a bank account. This was a key obstacle in the initial design of Digibank, which would have no physical presence or branches. How could new customers physically show their identification?

The digital team brainstormed how to resolve the problem. Those in Group Legal identified the solution. They proposed the biometric solution of collaborating with Café Coffee Day (an Indian café chain). This emphasized the importance of a whole organization being involved in understanding digitalization and its strategic objectives.

The digital team brainstormed how to resolve the problem. Those in Group Legal identified the solution.

DBS partnered with Café Coffee Day with its more than 600 outlets countrywide by placing a thumb reader in the Café Coffee Day branches. Each thumb reader cost $50, which cost considerably less than building a branch network! This way, new Digibank customers could go into a Café Coffee Day, order a cappuccino, and open an account within the targeted 90 seconds.

The Café Coffee Day solution was spurred on when team members realized almost every Indian had an "Aadhaar" card (individual identification number) that allows for biometric identification. The government had opened the use of the ID Card for everyday identification through thumbprints. By connecting through APIs, the government can authenticate the identity of a person, which is exactly what the bank required for KYC. To meet the ID requirement, the bank simply needed to capture thumb imprints.

When DBS launched Digibank in India in 2015, it faced a negative reaction from local bankers who tried to shut it down. But the ease of use created by the technology won over customers and won out against the local competition.

- **Validating Addresses Challenge**

In another early challenge, regulations in India stated that a new customer's address had to be validated so the bank could get in contact with that person. The consistent understanding in what the Digital Wave was aiming to achieve ensured alignment across all departments. This meant the Compliance Department was working with the new digital team to find solutions, not create obstacles. The compliance team solved this challenge by recognizing that, once new customers opened accounts, they had to receive their credit or debit cards. Activating the cards required

The compliance team solved this challenge by recognizing that, once new customers opened accounts, they had to receive their credit or debit cards.

entering a three-digit CCV into the app, thus confirming their addresses were valid. Even if customers had used their parents' addresses because they lived somewhere else, the fact of receiving the card and entering the code into the app meant the bank met the requirement of being able to get in touch with them.

- **Targeting the Right Customers**

Initially when Digibank launched, the bank focused on acquiring as many customers as quickly as possible to build momentum for its first-ever non-physical presence in a country. But as customers came on board, the bank identified that some customer profiles weren't an ideal fit. This led a focus on improved customer targeting, which then resulted in better customer acquisition and balances.

Altogether, Digibank has attracted more than 2.3 million customers and 650,000 saving accounts. It operates on one-fifth of the personnel head count needed in a traditional brick-and-mortar approach. This success in India soon led to the rollout of Digibank Indonesia.

In 2020, DBS amalgamated with Lakshmi Vilas Bank in India, which has accelerated the bank's growth trajectory in one of its key emerging markets.

2. Digibank Indonesia

In 2016, the bank set out to replicate India's Digibank success in Indonesia, the world's third largest country by population. This created a new set of challenges. For one, Indonesian regulations state that a bank must have employees.

Members of the T&O (Technology and Operations) team analyzed how they could support Digibank's expansion and which lessons it could learn from India's launch. They noted that everything in Indonesia was delivered by a motorbike. So instead of having coffee baristas as partners (as they did in India), they had "Gojek" (an Indonesian super app) drivers as employed bank tellers. Having a bank account arrive by a bike might seem strange, but in Indonesia, having *everything* delivered by bike is the norm, so why not your bank account?

The Gojek drivers were given authentication devices and became the bank's employees for KYC.

Adopting lessons from India's implementation and avoiding past mistakes, the bank's initial MVP was immediately a better version than in India. The learning curve had been shortened.

One key lesson was that, in the initial launch in India, the bank cast a broad net for customers. Anyone who spoke English and used a smartphone was a prospect, and the bank wanted all of them. However, they realized fairly quickly that they were attracting 18- to 25-year-olds. These young adults matched the requirements but did not have the capital or capacity for the bank to give them loans. Meanwhile, these young adults were taking advantage of the bank's free offers. So, when it launched Digibank in Indonesia, DBS switched its strategy from "net" fishing to a more targeted customer selection.

Another unique feature about Indonesia was that typically high interest rates attract customers to open accounts with a bank. But in Indonesia, this was not the case. The biggest driver of customer behavior was a gift. This highlighted the importance of learning distinctive consumer marketing behaviors for each market.

By applying the learning from Digibank India, DBS successfully implemented Digibank Indonesia in 12 months instead of 24 months. Indonesia's launch also helped in the continued improvement of the model for India.

3. Wealth Management iWealth App

As the bank became more customer obsessed and its technology DNA changed, significant changes were made in how its products were sold. In Wealth Management, Relationship Managers (RMs) were empowered to sell "open," which meant they not only offered DBS products but counseled clients on what services were specifically suited to them.

The new technology reinforced that the right product was sold to the right customer. For example, if a RM tried to sell a high-risk product to a person with a low-risk profile, the system would simply not allow it.

The Wealth Management team also wanted to map out how to serve customers differently by leveraging technology, so it set out to improve the Wealth Management app and launched the iWealth App in 2017.

The iWealth app was a digital wealth management platform that let customers manage and grow their wealth. At first, the team would ask for feedback whenever a user logged out. This provided a high rate of response as customers shared a vested interest in helping improve an app they frequently used. The Wealth Management team analyzed every piece of customer feedback. For example, when customers were using the iWealth app, they didn't want to have to log out in order to use the retail app. As a result of listening and acting on that feedback, iWealth was changed to allow retail transactions without having to shift to another app.

Wealth Management is a large user of a Treasury and Markets (T&M) digital platform called "Digi Markets" in which the bank can price and book deals. It can also access equity derivatives and compare prices with external competitors. This reinforced the goal of offering bank customers the best value. In addition, it allowed for FX (foreign exchange) and FX options and bonds all priced in real time, functions that had been processed manually only a few years ago. These changes continued to meet DBS customers' demand for instant pricing.

4. digiPortfolio

Part of the organization's journey has been to automate everything, resulting in the creation of digiPortfolio. This is a hassle-free, hybrid human-robo investment service that offers customers with as little as $1,000 the perfect match of human expertise and robo-technology. With it, they have an instant, cost-effective way to grow and protect their wealth through regional or global diversification. digiPortfolio taps into the best team of portfolio managers, whose expertise was previously accessible only to those with investment sums of $500,000 and above.

Besides carefully selecting exchange traded funds (ETFs) to create quality portfolios, the team monitors the market regularly, aligning digiPortfolio with the chief investment office's views. The goal is to ensure optimal asset allocation and portfolio resilience while initiating rebalancing when necessary.

digiPortfolio is coded to automate processes such as back-testing, rebalancing, and monitoring. By doing this, the bank can deliver scale and efficiency, while giving investors full transparency of their trade activities.

Over the last few years, the bank has seen dramatic growth in small-scale investors providing funds to invest in portfolios for them. This is a completely new source of business for DBS that could not have been done without digital capabilities in place.

5. Intelligent Banking

In 2020, DBS Bank doubled down on its Intelligent Banking capabilities across its digital banking services. These capabilities came at a time when customers were not only shifting to, but also sticking with, their mobile phones and online platforms for everyday banking needs.

The Intelligent Banking capabilities combined predictive analytics and customer-centric design to transform data into hyper-personalized, intuitive (and unintrusive) insights. These insights enabled customers to simplify how they managed their finances and investments. The Intelligent Banking engine has generated up to 13 million insights a month across its digital banking services. These have helped customers improve their financial planning, uncover blind spots in their monthly expenditures, and even make timely investment decisions. On the DBS iWealth app, for example, proactive triggers are sent to customers to alert them to foreign exchange pricing movements based on their portfolio holdings and previous activities.

The Intelligent Banking features are fueled by the bank's data science models. DBS tracks the customers' journeys and then presents real-time information to them based on what they are going through.

> "Through our Intelligent Banking capabilities, we have been laser-focused on delivering helpful and actionable insights that guide customers to make more informed financial and investment decisions—decisions that are even more crucial amid today's uncertainties. Our aim is to not only improve our

customers' finances, but also to ultimately be of tangible value to their lives." – *Seng Seng (Group Head of Consumer Banking and Wealth Management)*[12]

6. NAV Planner – a part of Intelligent Banking

NAV Planner is an intuitive digital tool that serves as a prime example of Intelligent Banking for customers.

NAV Planner helps customers track, protect, and grow their money in a way that works for them—not only for a day, month, or year, but as they go through life.

It provides customers with a budget tracker, suggestions on how to improve financial well-being, and an overview of their assets and liabilities. This planner grows with its user. Specifically, it:

- Provides a big picture of a customer's financial interests in one place
- Makes customers' money habits work for them by tracking and growing their investments
- Allows customers to chart their course to financial freedom by visualizing their retirement cashflow projection, highlighting any gaps they might need to fill, and seeing what trade-offs to make as they reach for their desired retirement lifestyle
- Automatically notifies customers when unusual or higher-than-normal bill payments are being made to ensure they don't accidentally overpay on any automated payments

12 "DBS doubles down on intelligent banking amid still-surging digital adoption," DBS.com accessed April 13, 2021, https://www.dbs.com/newsroom/DBS_doubles_down_on_intelligent_banking_amid_still_surging_digital_adoption.

About 2.2 million customers have engaged with this tool, providing more than 30 million financial planning insights. Almost 400,000 people have changed from net deficit to net positive, which means they have shifted from being borrowers to savers on the back of this budgeting and planning tool.

At the end of 2020, the bank launched SGFinDex, the world's first public-private open banking initiative. SGFinDex is a secure digital interface that links different banks in Singapore through open APIs, allowing them to share approved key information.

7. Digitalization of General and Life Insurance

Piyush challenged the bancassurance team to drive the digitalization of general and life insurance in the bank. The team adopted a two-pronged approach for adopting the Digital Wave. The goal was to enable employees to take advantage of digitalization, especially the RMs when working with a customer.

The team also wanted to leverage digitalization to offer products directly to customers. So, among other things, it created Mobile Protect to provide insurance for both new and used phones—a first in Singapore. For convenience, the product could be paid for using PayLah!.

After the launch of the Digital Wave, Your Financial Profile (YFP) became one of the bank's first digitalization ventures. At that time, the bancassurance team was assigned to enable RMs to deliver an enhanced customer experience. Using the YFP allowed RMs to better know their customers when sitting in front of them by including elements of KYC (Know Your Customer).

YFP had a STP connection to the life insurance company the bank partnered with. This meant complete information (e.g., illustration, application, fulfillment, and payments) could be displayed to customers on a computer screen. The insurance company then digitally received the information it needed to underwrite a policy, and within two days, the new policy was complete. The bancassurance specialist completed the process, then sent a secured PDF document with details to the customer.

YFP has since evolved into the RM Mobility app. This app allows RMs to check their schedules, make appointments, and track their business, thus making them more mobile than ever. As a result, sales of general insurance are gaining traction through the apps and online.

DBS customers today can have an omni presence, which means they can decide how much they want to do on their own versus how engaged they'd like to be with an RM. To provide information to customers and enable them to self-discover, insurance dashboards have been introduced. In addition, details about insurance policies are reflected on a customer's monthly statement.

Not surprisingly, the insurance side of DBS Bank has grown 15-fold over the past decade.

Internal Customer Examples

Many organizations focus their digital efforts on only the customer-facing components of the business.

Many organizations focus their digital efforts on only the customer-facing components of the business. But to successfully implement digitalization, every part of the organization has to be involved. When Digibank was launched, for example, Group Legal was the one who solved the problem of how to authenticate customers without having physical branches. This was one way Group Legal embraced the Digital Wave.

1. Group Legal Embraced the Digital Wave

Group Legal stressed the importance of understanding its customers' journeys (including its internal customers) and identified their pain points. They then adopted design thinking and new technologies to resolve these pain points. It took a scrum of Group Legal members to get together and agree on the journey for both external and internal customers in these areas:

- Compliance
- Compliance Training
- Fixing the "Plumbing"
- Legal Onboarding

Here are some resulting changes that enhanced the customer experience.

- **Shifting to Trusting Customers**

In 2017, the Legal and Compliance team focused on a critical customer journey—corporate customer onboarding. Team members reviewed the number of documents and questions being asked and redesigned the entire customer journey. They focused on reducing the amount of information a new customer had to submit by, for example, proactively extracting the required information from public sector data and conducting as much real-time processing as possible. They also pared down the questions to only those of importance to specific clients. This enabled the onboarding process to happen within a day.

This radical approach used reverse psychology. Instead of looking for a reason why a customer's business might be illegal, those in charge of onboarding would focus on proving that a customer was a *real* person operating a *real* business. They focused on identifying characteristics that reflected positively on a customer rather than only searching for the negative characteristics of a possibly dishonest company.

Today, they can run a profile that identifies a *real* person operating a *real* business with a reasonably high degree of confidence. All this allows for a smoother onboarding experience that Makes Banking Joyful.

- **Rethinking Compliance**

The Legal and Compliance team also focused on transforming compliance in ways that encouraged employees to want to comply with regulations rather than being forced to comply. Not an easy challenge. A prime example happened when the team could see from its internal data that employees looked up the do's and don'ts of travel from Singapore to Taiwan by reading 16,000-word compliance instructions on cross-border licensing. These employees took responsibility for being compliant themselves.

This is significant because when employees needed to discuss legal and compliance issues with their customers, they had a negative perspective that was far from joyful. So, to transform this area, Group Legal used design thinking to create a platform from which employees could select their business unit and their destination. After selections were made, a few simple guidelines would be revealed and questions like these were asked:

- Can you give a term sheet to the customer?
- Can you discuss products with the customer?

The employee would answer with a "yes" or "no."

As part of the transformation, the team fostered a "peer culture" in which all employees in the bank were treated the same, no matter their level. The goal was to create a positive experience with various stakeholders as well as to redesign service standards and eventually achieve operational excellence. The challenge was to demonstrate that, within the team, the skills, commitment, and funding were available to achieve their transformation.

- **Rethinking Compliance Training**

The team also addressed changing the way the bank's Legal and Compliance areas trained its colleagues. Specifically, they shifted from technical face-to-face training on legal requirements to understanding what to do in behavioral situations.

Employees used to attend three-hour legal and compliance training sessions that, with travel, would consume half a day. Throughout the training, their focus was to *learn enough to pass an exam* rather than to *ensure correct behavior*. In implementing the Digital Wave, the approach changed from classroom training to online learning using fact-based scenarios. This allowed employees to make one of three decisions:

- To approve on their own authority
- To decline on their own authority
- To escalate

In the team's view, these were the only decisions required. All training could be designed around this simple selection: yes, no, or escalate.

This approach brought about a number of cultural challenges for the legal and compliance teams, but two main benefits prevailed: First, eliminating the cost of face-to-face classroom training, and second (and more important), training for behaviors rather than technical content.

2. An Employee's Onboarding Customer Journey

Over the last few years, DBS has grown from 18,000 to more than 30,000 employees. HR adopted customer journey thinking to improve the process of joining the bank and to view the journey from a new hire's perspective. The HR team recognized significant opportunities, including:

- Speaking often to new hires in their first three months of joining the team
- Preparing the infrastructure for new hires to be ready on their first day
- Making sure that managers were cascading the goals effectively

Desiring a positive customer journey for new hires resulted in HR building a platform that allowed for digital onboarding of documents. It also centralized certain processes to make them more seamless and easier for managers to use when preparing for new hires.

Today, new employees are connected to the DBS platform *before* their first day on the job so they can engage with the bank. Specifically, they can check out what's going on to familiarize themselves with the organization ahead of time.

Today, new employees are connected to the DBS platform *before* their first day on the job so they can engage with the bank.

On their first day, new hires spend the morning with an HR representative who provides an overview of the bank's culture, programs, and products. After the orientation, new employees collect their computers and mobile phones so they can be productive from day one. They also have immediate preapproved access to the relevant data for their job.

At the end of days 45, 90, and 180, the new hires complete a survey to ensure the onboarding experience has been both smooth and joyful.

3. Addressing Pain Points and the Future of Work

The term "Future of Work" has been used in the bank for years to acknowledge and address the pain points employees face every day. It focuses on both the tools employees have as well the culture they work in.

Despite initially not having the best tools, some employees still managed to navigate around the difficulties and accomplished great things. At the same time, other employees were frustrated with the workplace and had better experiences outside of work. Some were also having better experiences as customers (all employees are also bank customers) than when they came to work and used the bank's systems.

DBS declared 2019 as the year of the employee and set out to invest time and money fixing the gaps between employee and customer experiences. As part of this goal, a program was initiated in which each country identified its own pain points and rectified them. For example, in Hyderabad, India, the bank had a dress code that allowed employees to wear whatever they liked as long as it did not embarrass their parents. Inspired by a Netflix policy, Hyderabad set policies that treated and respected people as adults. Its people responded positively to them.

DBS declared 2019 as the year of the employee and set out to invest time and money fixing the gaps between employee and customer experiences.

Recognizing that policies and procedures were issues, the bank established a committee to address them. The approach was called "kiasu committee." (Kiasu is a local Singapore term meaning "having a fear of missing out," similar to the term FOMO [fear of missing out] in America.) This meant any employee in the organization could request a change to a policy or procedure. The committee, made up of both junior and senior employees and chaired by the head of legal compliance, acted as a jury. If committee members agreed with the employee, then the person responsible for the policy or procedure would be asked to change it.

The bank also turned its attention to another pain point—travel expenses. Using its 4Ds framework, it discovered the "job to be done" was to ensure employees were not out of pocket for travel, given the long time it took to get reimbursed. After conducting a customer journey for employees, DBS identified travel expenses as a toil issue and quickly recognized it as an emotional one, too. People clearly didn't want to wait a long time for reimbursements! The solution? The bank partnered with Grab (a ride-hailing service) that invoiced the bank directly. This eliminated employees paying for their own travel.

Another example involved the "Tell Piyush" ritual when, once a quarter, anyone can communicate with Piyush, and he personally responds. Numerous messages to Piyush identified a frustration from employees about wasting time traveling to meet their bosses located in a different office. This resulted in the bank further investing in video conferencing, which eliminated

Another example involved the "Tell Piyush" ritual when, once a quarter, anyone can communicate with Piyush, and he personally responds.

travel time, took toil out of the system, and was well received by employees.

In late 2020, the bank announced a range of initiatives to further embrace the future of work. These included:

- Employees were given flexibility to work remotely for up to 40% of the time.
- Upskilling agenda was accelerated with 7,200 employees scheduled to be trained.
- Deployment of data-driven agile squads was scaled up.

A critical success factor of the Digital Wave was the launch of ecosystems in the bank, discussed in the next chapter.

CHAPTER 11
Building Ecosystems

Prior to the Digital Wave, the bank's business model was based on a network of branches, data centers, and customer reach through multiple products and services. But it had become increasingly important in this hypercompetitive world for organizations to scale up by leveraging the capabilities of partners.

DBS bank now focuses its business model on building ecosystems because banking can no longer stand alone in a connected world. Today's technology advancements allow gathering and analyzing detailed customer data while providing new kinds of connectivity to enhance its customers' journeys.

In DBS's research paper "Pivot or Perish: Ecosystem, the emerging business model,"[13] an ecosystem is defined as: "Bringing together entities in disparate industries to create new offerings or capture value that individual organizations or sectors may not be capable of creating on their own. Through ecosystems, marketers gain the ability to cater to customer needs, without prompting the customer to look further than the company for a product."

13 DBS, "Pivot or Perish: Ecosystem, the emerging business model," DBS.com, January 10, 2019, https://www.dbs.com/aics/templatedata/article/generic/data/en/GR/012019/190110_insights_blackbook_pivot_or_perish.xml.

Beginning of Ecosystems in DBS

In 2012, bank leaders were already questioning how to connect different systems to improve customers' experience. Outside the bank, people were talking about APIs (Application Programming Interfaces), but many bankers did not know what they were or could not see their potential. As DBS moved first to microservices and then to ecosystems, APIs grew rapidly in importance.

APIs that enable building ecosystems *externally* are about connectivity; *internally* they are about both control and connectivity. A team needs to have control of "who can do what internally" because the person given the responsibility for operating the API and scaling up the business must be held accountable. Internally, an extra layer of control is required. At DBS, employees aren't allowed to make changes on their own. (This differs from the norm in DevOps, in which one person does have control.)

APIs have become a significant driver of business growth, creating new value to a business for two reasons: 1) they offer customers a more embedded experience and 2) they reveal more data for analysis.

By 2017, the bank's leadership team had reached two conclusions. First, it recognized the need to shift its thinking. That meant to be a digital player, leadership had to be open to partnering with other organizations and could not play by itself. Second, it deeply appreciated how customers *didn't* start their journey from

APIs have become a significant driver of business growth, creating new value to a business for two reasons: 1) they offer customers a more embedded experience and 2) they reveal more data for analysis.

the bank. This awareness aligned with its work focused on a customer's "job to be done."

These two conclusions also recognized that millions of impressions, clicks, and engagements were being made *outside* the bank. If the bank couldn't connect to these potential partners, then it was missing massive amounts of data and customer knowledge as well as future opportunities.

As mentioned earlier, in 2017, the bank launched the world's largest banking API platform, going live with more than 150 APIs. Today, it has more than 1,000 APIs and over 400 partners. The organization's fast cadence demonstrates to external partners how quick and responsive the bank has become. For example, DBS collaborates with Tally (which provides enterprise resource planning software) in India. Tally has more than eight million SME customers. Why does Tally not work with a local Indian bank? Because it tried and the partnership failed. Its leaders have learned that DBS's API structure, fast cadence, and agility not only allow it to improve its customer offering, but also increase the bank's credibility. This helps attract new partners for DBS as well as top talent.

The organization's fast cadence demonstrates to external partners how quick and responsive the bank has become.

POC Framework

To guide the development of ecosystems with partners and understand the new approach, DBS adopted a three-stage framework called POC:

- **P** means **Participate** with other platforms where DBS comes through as a participant on an external party's platform or ecosystem. For example, the bank strategically invested in Carousel (a site for buying and selling goods) as part of its DBS PayLah! platform.
- **O** means **Orchestrate** where the bank is the platform and brings on board partners and multiple players. For example, a customer can now buy or sell a car on the bank's website, work out a worry-free home purchase plan, select an electricity provider, or book flights and hotels. By using DBS PayLah!, the bank also orchestrates payments to third parties for such items as movie tickets and insurance.
- **C** means **Create** in a complete white space. This is where no real player is out there; instead, the bank initiates the platform. An example of a created app is Smart Buddy, which has morphed into an educational ecosystem.

Entry into Successful Marketplaces

DBS sought to make banking more seamless and joyful for customers when purchasing property. Today, it also sells cars and holidays. Just a few years ago, imagine what consumers would have thought about buying a car from their bank!

- **Property Marketplace**

Singapore has a vibrant property market. Launching a new Property Marketplace platform allowed the bank to be more innovative in offering adjacent services beyond mortgages, including insurance and renovation loans.

Today, customers can browse online to find multiple property agents and sites. With its mortgage calculator, Property

Marketplace helps them make early-stage calculations on mortgages so they can weigh their options. They can also acquire Approval in Principle and facilitate other aspects of their mortgage journeys.

- **Car Marketplace**

The government of Singapore places a high tax on cars (called Certificate of Entitlement or COE). Therefore, approximately 90 percent of car purchases require a loan, which serves to limit the number of cars on the roads. To discourage people from buying cars, the country has an excellent, safe, and reliable public transport system. In Singapore, for example, if a train breaks down at any time, its operator is penalized by the government!

Still, Singaporeans want to own cars. Thus, customers' need to get loans led to car sellers being paid a high commission when they recommended a bank. The bank, in turn, depended on car sellers for their recommendations. When purchasing a car, thinking about the loan or insurance is not typically a top-of-mind consideration. The Consumer team recognized this as an excellent opportunity to examine the customer journey as well as show empathy to their customers and apply design thinking.

In 2017, an agile squad reimagined the customer journey and created the launch of the Car Marketplace, a first of its kind in Singapore. It was a platform that centralized customer search efforts for a car with all the different steps easy to access on one website. The launch of Car Marketplace required Singapore's central bank's approval since it fell outside of a bank's traditional and approved parameter.

As a consumer, Car Marketplace allows you to search for and buy your dream car or sell one you don't want. When buying, the site lets you calculate your budget, view dealers, or buy directly from a seller. When selling a car, the site allows you to price your car and sell it fast. It guides you through the transaction in three steps.

The site also recommends insurance and offers purchase of roadside assistance and accessories. It also features recommended articles to read before buying and selling goods.

Immediately after the Car Marketplace launch, the bank's customers realized a significant reduction in the cost of acquiring car loans and insurance as well as an efficient back-end process. Today, DBS's Car Marketplace is the largest direct seller-to-buyer car market in Singapore.

> "DBS Car Marketplace exemplifies how we are reimagining banking using digital technology and innovation to extend our reach. Our insights indicate that consumers increasingly value transparency and simplicity, particularly in large purchases such as cars." – *Jeremy (Head of DBS Consumer Banking Group in Singapore)*[14]

- **Travel Marketplace**

Travel Marketplace is the bank's first payments-enabled marketplace. It was also Singapore's first one-stop integrated travel marketplace in partnership with Singapore Airlines, Expedia Partner Solutions, and Chubb Insurance.

The Travel Marketplace offers travelers competitive flight fares, hotel rates, and free travel insurance coverage for more than 25,000 holiday destinations worldwide.

---

14 "DBS partners sgCarMart and Carro to create Singapore's largest direct buyer-to-seller car marketplace," DBS.com, accessed April 14, 2021, https://www.dbs.com/newsroom/DBS_partners_sgCarMart_and_Carro_to_create_Singapores_largest_direct_buyer_to_seller_car_marketplace.

- **Electricity Marketplace**

Through the bank's Digibank app, heads of households can search for utility price plans best suited to their electricity consumption. This app is aimed at making life simpler for customers while enjoying a savings on their bills.

Platform Is the New Product

The Digital Wave drove the move from product to platform across the bank. The move focused on scope and scale—from developing the best products to developing the best networks. For an example of a platform, consider how Apple launched the iPhone as a product in 2007 and how today it operates as a platform with over two million applications available in its App Store.

The bank's move from product to platform came with these three challenges:

1. **Acquiring customers through partners.** Going further upstream in the customer journey created more opportunities to capture new customers through partners. When a consumer wants to buy a car, for example, the loan can come from DBS. This is even more critical in the markets where DBS has little physical presence (such as in India and Indonesia) and fully depends on digitalization to connect with its customers. By working together, both parties reduce their cost of customer acquisition.
2. **Gathering non-traditional data from partners to make credit decisions.** The bank gathers data on its customers. The non-traditional data it has on customers provides more accuracy, granularity, and actionable data for making decisions. For customers new to banking or credit, it is imperative to have other sources of data (this can come

from travel patterns, telco data, or other external sources) to be able to make decisions on lending. To access this sort of data, DBS has to partner with related firms that then become part of its ecosystem.

3. **Enhancing product offerings through partners.** Collaborating with partners unlocks greater revenue opportunities from customers that the bank did not access before. For example, previously, DBS would only enter the house-buying customer journey in terms of the mortgage application process. Today, its Property Marketplace provides listings from partners. It also smooths out the customer journey by integrating the mortgage calculation and affordability assessment into the experience.

Early partnering successes for DBS came by integrating the bank's APIs with Singapore's Golden Village (cinema), followed by Singapore's Carousel (buying and selling goods) and GoJek (car-hailing service).

Building Ecosystem Partnerships

Building successful ecosystem partnerships requires an investment in time, mutual commitment, and openness to collaboration. It also takes resilience and belief to build traction and reach inflection points. To this day, as DBS improves the customer journey, it can be challenging for the bank and its partners to identify an equitable value exchange.

The ecosystem partnerships that work best happen when both parties benefit from working together more or less equally. Each partner must also share a mutual commitment to offering customers a better experience as well as being open about data collaboration.

As the bank advances its efforts in connecting adjacencies, its aim of Making Banking Joyful becomes embedded in its customers' lives.

A pain point that the bank has been able to address for both consumer and corporate customers is KYC while onboarding. For corporate customers, this process used to take an average of 45 days in the industry. But now, by making the procedure seamless and paperless by adopting digital signatures and with open APIs, the bank has reduced it to under six days. Traditionally, this process involved submitting numerous physical documents and multiple iterations between the bank and the customer onboarding. The use of AI and machine learning eliminates duplication and manual processing.

Supply Chain Digitalization

The application of API technologies has provided DBS with the capacity to work with its partners to digitalize various supply chains. This has enabled the bank to not only embed itself into other organizations but into the entire industry in a way that could not happen before digitalization. A prime example is for logistic supply in food and beverage, which the bank is rapidly able to integrate through APIs.

When conducting supply chains through APIs, the bank can do prominence tracking. In this way, it is establishing its own rubber exchange and using blockchain technology to track the source of the commodity. It also collaborates with other providers, such as Google, to make sure sustainability information regarding the supply chain goes back to the state.

In late 2020, the bank launched the world's first integrated digital exchange, backed by a traditional bank.

CHAPTER 12

Ecosystems Examples

The success of two of the bank's early adoptions of ecosystems helped build momentum. They are DBS PayLah! and POSB Smart Buddy.

1. DBS PayLah!

DBS PayLah! is the bank's digital wallet for its Singapore customers. Initiated in 2014, it set out to become Singapore's favorite digital wallet. Initially built as a mobile app, it focused on peer-to-peer payments at first. The country's smaller size acted as a moat to keep out competition, so the bank considered digital payments in Singapore "theirs to lose."

In 2014, DBS set about responding to the rising challenge across Asia from Alibaba, WeChat, and the global Fintech movement that was changing the way payments were made. The bank wanted to be first to market in Singapore and a leader in defining the landscape. Being one of the incumbents with the largest consumer base allowed it to design the optimal solution for its customers. That way, DBS leaders could set their own agenda rather than having it determined for them.

- **Transforming to Digital Payments in Singapore**

Launching a digital wallet involved changing customers' habits. Initially, having a digital wallet did not have enough perceived value to break the habit of using cash, so it failed to pass the toothbrush test—a system used at least once a day.

DBS PayLah!'s failed "toothbrush test" led the bank to rethink how to change customer habits. In turn, this led to offering merchant payments and adding bill payments, donations, pre-paid top-ups, and online checkout. PayLah!'s success shows how essential it is for every part of the organization to have the same purpose and to be open to new ways of doing business, even though a change may initially eliminate revenue streams.

To ensure adoption of a digital wallet, these three strategic decisions were made:

1. The new digital wallet system had to sit with one of the vertical businesses to avoid any cannibalization standing in the way of driving adoption. For example, the credit card and digital wallet businesses could have ended up competing if every digital wallet transaction was cannibalizing the existing credit card business. DBS PayLah! overcame that.
2. The team targeted the cash transaction segment rather than, for example, the high-value luxury items segment. Thereby, the team avoided trying to do too much. The team also focused on how to gain traction with the new mode by putting it in places that could displace cash transactions at traditionally cash-heavy businesses.

These places included taxis, on student campuses, and at "hawker centers" (Singapore food courts).

3. The team adopted agile methodology. This meant creating a group with members from different businesses such as cards, regional offices, channels, and deposits. Their focus was to make DBS PayLah! the most successful digital wallet in Singapore. By assigning the team responsibility for decisions, the iteration became faster, accelerated the move from product thinking to agile, and helped overcome an issue faced early on—that outsiders brought in to help digitize the bank were treated differently than employees. This had set up an "us versus them" mentality. Today, all teams collaborate as a result of an evolution that took three to four years.

Contributing to the success of DBS PayLah! was senior management's support and investment.

Also, at this time, the bank stopped using the term "e-channels," as it recognized it was selling almost completely through its digital platform. The term used today is "e-business," and that was eventually simplified into "digital," "Web" and "mobile." As the bank's digital awareness evolved, the term "channels" became obsolete. Products being provided digitally became regarded as digital products in their own right. For example, DBS Remit allows customers in Singapore to remit money overseas, has 99 percent of its transactions online, and is completely STP (Straight-Through Processing). Using STP, the transfer is complete in seconds, and the remitting party receives instant confirmation. As the engagement is online, REMIT is no longer called a channel but the product itself. In 2019, REMIT transaction volume grew more than 50 percent a year. By 2020, REMIT generated over $100 million.

As the thinking evolved, employees stopped designing for "online" versus "offline"—that is, what was offered through physical branches. Today, everything is customer-focused solution and digital-first.

- **DBS PayLah! Adoption in Singapore**

The inflection point for DBS PayLah! came when QR codes started gaining traction in Singapore, especially among young customers who had not been conditioned to using credit cards. The team had installed a QR code feature into the product about six months ahead of that inflection point, thereby allowing DBS PayLah! to gain wallet share quickly when the domestic network "NETS" (Network for Electronic Transfers, a cashless payment system) launched QR code acceptance in 2017. The QR code feature was also a factor when, shortly after, the government issued guidelines to drive the adoption and harmonization of QR codes.

In 2016, DBS PayLah! became more readily adopted and grew exponentially. This led to the building of a "super app" in Singapore in 2018. Before long, DBS PayLah! evolved into a lifestyle app with frequent use that more than beat the toothbrush test.

With DBS PayLah! positioned as a digital wallet and viewed as a product rather than a payment tool, the Consumer bank team first struggled to clarify this positioning in the overall bank's offerings, given other payment methods already in play (e.g., credit cards, Apple Pay, internet banking, etc.) and what each of those products represented to customers. Even today, DBS is constantly improving and harmonizing the various payment propositions available to its customers. Given the differing unique value propositions, the bias tends to be letting *customers* choose the best method.

Today, the digital wallet allows customers to easily buy movie tickets, do their shopping, earn mall reward points, make restaurant reservations, and pay for rides—with more uses continually being added. This helps the bank understand its customers more deeply and provides frequently improving customer journeys. At the same time, it also allows the bank to gather data on its customers. For example, you reserve a table on DBS PayLah! and 30 minutes before the reservation, it uses predictive analytics to ask you if you want to hail a ride to the restaurant.

Today, DBS PayLah! has almost two million users.

- **Ang Bao (Red Packets) Go Virtual**

During the Chinese New Year period in 2019, the Consumer bank piloted the first loadable QR Ang Bao (red packets containing cash, given out at Chinese New Year) in the world. With this loadable QR Ang Bao, customers were able to preserve the Chinese New Year tradition of gifting but without using physical cash.

The giver of QR Ang Bao loads the value into the QR Ang Bao using DBS PayLah! Then the receiver simply uses the app to scan and receive the Ang Bao money gift.

- **DBS PayLah! Wave Crashed the System on Singapore's National Day**

In the early stages of rolling out DBS PayLah!, the team noticed an entertainment event on TV in China that involved participants opening WeChat and waving a cell phone. The team in Singapore copied the idea and set up a promotion called $100,000 SGWave. On Singapore's National Day in 2015, people could win instant cash by waving their phones in a certain manner at predetermined times. The team advertised this SGWave both online and in traditional media, encouraging people to wave for National Day using the DBS PayLah! app.

What happened? The app entries were so numerous that the system crashed! The reason for the crash was that the spike in volume registered as a hack, causing all of DBS PayLah! to shut down. The executives' reaction? "Okay, we tried. Now fix it, learn from it, and move on." In other organizations, someone may have been fired. In this case, the executives' reaction reinforced DBS's experimentation and learning culture.

Today, the Consumer and Institutional Banking Group businesses are studying how to integrate their payments gateway so corporate customers can manage consumer payments across a seamless gateway and vice versa. The end game is data self-serve or N=1. That means not needing to ask permission to use data and accessing what's required to improve one's job. N=1 means customers see the right products at the right time when they want or need them. It also identifies each customer's notification preferences, such as via messages on the app or via email.

Although this result is complicated to achieve, this DBS team is working on N=1 as another way to improve the customer journey.

- **Ecosystem Partners**

DBS PayLah! has evolved into an ecosystem as it adopts APIs. Although partnering with other organizations was initially not natural for banks, it became part of the new mindset and approach for digitalization.

The bank targets various ecosystem partners that offer customers greater value while encouraging increased use of DBS PayLah! Its partnership with Singapore's Comfort Delgro taxi company, for example, was an early success that improved adoption.

The bank also targeted the food vertical (one of Singapore's favorite activities) on the National University of Singapore's campus. Once again, DBS PayLah! traction increased, which got students in the habit of using a stored value facility.

Another ecosystem partner is GOJEK. In mid-2019, DBS and GOJEK (a transportation network and logistics start-up company in Jakarta, Indonesia) collaborated to add DBS PayLah! options to its driver hailing service. According to GOJEK, about 35 percent of its daily ride-hailing transactions are paid for in cash. The ecosystem partnership allowed users who did not own a debit or credit card to use an alternative to paying cash and to use digital payment.

This partnership allowed payment to be deposited directly into a GOJEK driver's account by leveraging DBS's IDEAL RAPID, a straight-through API solution.

The bank is aiming to more than double its DBS PayLah! users to 3.5 million by 2023. It will do this by building on the three Ps—Payments, Partners, and Platform—as part of a long-term strategic road map.

2. POSB Smart Buddy

At the start of the implementation of the Digital Wave, Piyush was driving every part of the bank to challenge the status quo and think differently. As part of its responses to the CEO's challenge, the Consumer bank addressed the customer pain point of parents scrambling in the morning to give their children lunch money. The solution eventually resulted in Singapore children eating less sugar!

Adopting agile methodology, the team developed a wearable watch for schoolchildren that let parents pass children their lunch money digitally. It's called the Smart Buddy. To create this app, the agile squad experimented over an intense 18-month period using pilots at three schools.

As mentioned earlier, digitalization is not always about inventing a product but about creating a platform. In this case, giving schoolchildren a wearable watch for digital credit was useless if vendors could not accept their payments. So, the team went to individual food and beverage vendors at participating schools and encouraged them to adopt cashless transactions.

As mentioned earlier, digitalization is not always about inventing a product but about creating a platform.

- **Interface with Facebook Messenger**

During the pilot in 2016, though, the team realized numerous food and beverage vendors had their own apps. Finding, downloading, and using different apps was not attractive to them. To resolve the problem of being inundated with apps, the team pivoted to Facebook Messenger, which most of their customers used. Facebook Messenger now lists all the different vendors participating at the children's schools.

In August 2017, POSB Smart Buddy was launched as a contactless payment ecosystem to cultivate sensible saving and spending habits among students in an interactive, engaging way. It not only resolved the issue of parents scrambling to give the children lunch money; it also tracked what food items their children were buying at school.

Smart Buddy analytics revealed the kids' eating habits, paving the way for parents to educate their children on eating right and spending money wisely. The Singapore government became interested in Smart Buddy, as it was looking to improve eating habits among children. The data also translated into defining trends and discovering insights.

Since Smart Buddy's launch, more than 29,000 schoolchildren have been using the free wearable watch, and 62 schools have joined the initiative.

The success of Smart Buddy became an early catalyst for the Consumer team to rethink its whole consumer offering, shifting from selling products to creating platforms. Smart Buddy is not a digital wallet product; it is a platform that interconnects customers (schoolchildren) with vendors. In Singapore, those vendors also include libraries and bookstores. Not only does Smart Buddy allow parents to track their children's eating and buying habits, but it also gives the Singapore Health Promotion Board (HPB) data that can help reduce sugar intake for school children. HPB provides nutrition tips that encourage healthy living.

CHAPTER 13

Customer Trust

DBS had been focusing on the interaction between system performance and customer journey behavior. Simultaneously, it had been examining customer journeys to see where bankers could predict behavior. Bringing these two ideas together became known as Customer Science.

To make joyful experiences, the bank uses Customer Science to create instruments and methods of observation that help it track customer journeys. Specifically, it combines customer behavior data with systems data to build real-time analytical models.

To make joyful experiences, the bank uses Customer Science to create instruments and methods of observation that help it track customer journeys.

Customer Science Concept

Using a concept adopted from Netflix, the bank first tested Customer Science on Digibank by monitoring customer behavior on the app. It also created a full-time customer operation unit in India that tracked customer journeys in real time. This allowed the bank to preempt and predict systems issues so it could resolve them—even before they happened!

For example, the data revealed the Digibank app in India had login issues. Using Customer Science, the team monitored the login failures and identified the system wasn't at fault; it was a customer behavior issue. Specifically, the app's password format was different than what was commonly used in India, which caused a high login error rate. The solution? The bank standardized the login and made password recovery and reset easier. As a result, the login success rate jumped from mid-60 to mid-90 percent. These changes have also been applied to Digibank Indonesia.

The concept started by bank leaders asking, "What does Operations need to do for DBS to contribute to becoming the best bank in the world?" Part of the answer was to develop data instrumentation.

Data Instrumentation

The key question is not *what* gets measured but *how*. Data instrumentation put in place the right measures and tracking that DBS employees could use to identify how to improve customer journeys.

Examining data-led models helps prevent issues from occurring and keeps customers engaged profitably so the bank can deepen its relationship with them.

The key question is not *what* gets measured but *how*.

Data instrumentation is set up in an operations control center to monitor customer journeys in real time. The center's

Every organization has data, and the data from the DBS data instrumentation has become a key tool to nudge customer behavior.

system gathers behavioral and device performance data to anticipate and solve potential issues by assisting the customer through SMS, email, or chatbots. The data-led models have also enabled the bank to create hyper-personalized solutions based on customers' needs. They do this by contextually introducing products and solutions relevant to customers at the right time.

Every organization has data, and the data from the DBS data instrumentation has become a key tool to nudge customer behavior. Here are two examples:

- **Nudge Customers toward Self-Servicing Channels**

Data instrumentation was adopted at the contact center to predict customer servicing needs and nudge customers toward self-servicing channels, e.g., chatbots. The data assisted in reducing inbound calls and improving response time. (In 2020, chatbot usage volume increased from 350,000 to 400,000 unique conversations, with 82 percent of requests self-fulfilled by customers.)

The Customer Center in Singapore historically has processed over four million inbound customer calls every year, but the bank now continues to see call volumes drop as customers are able to find answers to their questions on their own.

The Customer Center transformation involved reskilling over 500 employees to take on 13 new job roles. These included, for example, employees becoming voice biometrics specialists, live chat agents, and customer experience designers.

Data and digital dashboards were also used to map a customer's journey. For example, by using behavioral and device performance data, the Customer Center team could anticipate and solve potential issues such as failed card transactions or a card retained in an ATM. The team could then assist customers via SMS, email, or chatbot.

- **Nudge Customers to Plan for Retirement**

The bank developed a retirement planning software called Face Your Future. Using facial recognition software and artificial intelligence, it can paint a visual portrait of what customers may look like when they reach retirement. This software has been aimed at customers as a nudge to plan for their retirement. In addition, Face Your Future's algorithm is able to predict a person's retirement expenses based on his or her desired lifestyle.

Responsibility for Protecting Customer Data

DBS Bank, of course, takes data protection seriously. In addition to each country's regulations, the bank is thoughtful about:

- What is appropriate to do with data
- How customers feel about their data
- Definitions they/we use
- How they think about appropriateness
- How they think about suitability
- Who should be allowed to access the data
- The roles of people

To oversee its responsible use of data, DBS leaders introduced the PURE Framework. The acronym PURE stands for:

- **P**urposeful – Data use should be purposeful.
- **U**nsurprising – Data use should be expected by individuals.
- **R**espectful – Data use should be respectful toward individuals, taking into consideration social norms.
- **E**xplainable – Data use should be explainable and justifiable.

For example, when the bank uses third-party data, it must tell its customers it is doing so to comply with PURE policy. When collecting data, employees are required to ask and answer these questions:

- Did we inform the customer what we will be using the data for?
- Will the data use be unsurprising to everyone involved?
- Will the bank use the data respectfully and purposefully?
- Can the data use and results be explained?
- If customers ask why they have been targeted and why and how their data is used, are we able to answer them with confidence?

Customer trust is a core component of the Digital Wave, which the bank takes to heart.

Questions for Consideration

1. What does customer obsession mean to your organization?
2. How can you become more customer obsessed?
3. What needs to change in your leader's mindset to transform to digital?
4. How do you ensure the decisions being made across the organization are customer centric?
5. What are the most important "jobs to be done" for your customers?
6. What products and services should you no longer offer as you transform to digital?
7. How can you adopt customer journey mapping?
8. How can you identify and solve pain points in your customer journeys?
9. How can you adopt and leverage design thinking?
10. How can you collect the required data to improve customer journeys?
11. How do you ensure customers' trust in using their data?
12. How can you develop the right ecosystems?

CHAPTER 14

Third Strategy Principle of Digital Wave:

Culture by Design, and Think Like a Start-Up

When the Digital Wave was launched, the leaders questioned how the culture needed to transform to support the implementation. Was it about speed, agile, customer focus, innovation, or something else?

Culture by Design

To explore that question, the bank launched Culture by Design, a program that identified what needed to change to implement the Digital Wave.

Culture by Design started by examining future goals for the bank, then identified any blocks to achieving them. Then the team ran experiments to learn how to overcome those blocks. The experiments were as simple as a change in vocabulary or as complex as a whole new policy or process.

A key outcome was that the bank wanted to imitate the culture of a start-up organization. Today, DBS's desire to innovate is in its DNA—just as it would be for a start-up.

> Culture by Design started by examining future goals for the bank, then identified any blocks to achieving them.

To develop this kind of culture, the leadership team critically defined five characteristics, captured under the acronym ABCDE, which have been thoroughly woven into its DNA. They are:

- **A**gile
- **B**e a learning organization
- **C**ustomer obsessed
- **D**ata driven
- **E**xperiment and take risks

These five characteristics are explained in their own chapters following this one.

Previously, changes made under the Asia Wave had started to transform DBS's culture, yet more changes were required to make the Digital Wave successful. The Asia Wave culture transformation had helped leaders and employees have an open attitude toward change. This laid the essential groundwork for its transformation to a start-up culture.

Largest Roadblock to a Start-up Culture

An early question the bank's leadership asked was: "What is the biggest roadblock to transform the organization into a start-up culture?" What did they identify as the number-one blocker to

"What is the biggest roadblock to transform the organization into a start-up culture?"

transformation? The way meetings were conducted in the bank. Too many meetings were held, too many were ineffective, and too many had no stated purpose. This led to an experiment that gave birth to MOJO.

MOJO

MOJO was the name of the organization-wide movement to run effective meetings across the whole bank. Its goal was to make the best use of everyone's time.

MO stands for the Meeting Owner, who has three responsibilities:

- State the purpose and context of the meeting.
- Summarize key points of the meeting at the end.
- Ensure everyone has an equal voice so that collective intelligence can be leveraged.

JO stands for the Joyful Observer, whose responsibilities are to:

- Keep track of time.
- Commit to giving honest feedback to the MO on how well he or she performed.

If a MO receives too much negative feedback, he or she is no longer allowed to organize meetings.

As a result, having MOJO at each meeting more than doubled its effectiveness. Specifically, MOJO ensured meetings started and finished on time, thus saving more than 500,000 employee hours. By the JO giving frequent feedback, employees could adopt that feedback conscientiously. Because of this practice, the bank increased its ability to provide and leverage feedback as a tool for improvement. In addition, the percentage of employees who say they have an equal share of voice in meetings has increased dramatically from 40 to 90 percent.

Specifically, MOJO ensured meetings started and finished on time, thus saving more than 500,000 employee hours.

Initially, meeting rooms displayed signs and other collateral to remind employees to use MOJO. Signage also appeared around office areas to prompt employees to adopt MOJO. Today, they receive digital nudges. Every month, MOs receive a feedback report from JOs via email regarding their performance.

Everyone at DBS has adopted this MOJO practice when in meetings, including Piyush. He himself has been called out by JOs when demonstrating less than positive behavior! This happened in a meeting when the JO told the CEO he was not taking time to hear other opinions in the room. Piyush, an excellent role model, thanked the JO for the feedback and gave him encouragement. News of this incident spread around the bank, which encouraged others to adopt the right meeting behavior.

Consider the kind of culture that allows an employee to give the CEO negative feedback and to be praised for it! This allows the JO to feel psychologically safe, which is critical for the desired team and culture development.

The bank even developed a MOJO app (not a surprise) available to the public (perhaps a surprise) at www.meetingmojo.co. In addition to explaining the roles, the app provides a MOJO Productivity Timer. This features an automatic buzzer at 10 and 5 minutes before the meeting ends. It also provides a series of alerts to remind JOs to give feedback and a final alert to wrap up the meeting.

Improving the quality of meetings has significantly contributed to a positive culture at DBS and has improved the effectiveness of daily operations. Most important, it has freed up employees' time to focus on more value-adding activities.

Joy Space

Another critical culture component was the bank's working environment. Creating the right culture requires an environment that supports the desired cultural behaviors. For DBS, this led to developing Joy Spaces.

The term "Joy Space" refers to the bank's building portfolio that called for open-plan collaborative spaces to revolutionize the working environment. In addition, DBS encouraged agile and other desired behaviors articulated in the Culture by Design program.

Inspired by GANDALF organizations, the bank rolled out spaces with free seating that focused on collaboration, making the cultural transformation to agile highly visible. It also provided the right environment in conjunction with new working practices. For example, when employees had an issue to resolve, they pulled together a scrum and found an area in the open space to discuss it, including sitting on the floor if required. This configuration supported ending the lingering silo mentality while encouraging an agile culture.

Inspired by GANDALF organizations, the bank rolled out spaces with free seating that focused on collaboration, making the cultural transformation to agile highly visible.

PRIDE!

Throughout the transformation of all three strategic waves, the bank's values have continued to underpin the culture and drive acceptable behaviors.

The PRIDE! values have shaped the way the bank conducted business and how employees collaborated with each other. The values are:

- Purpose-driven
- Relationship-led
- Innovative
- Decisive
- Everything Fun!

They recognize and celebrate the contribution and success of others. They are open-minded, empathetic, and respectful of others. In doing so, they create a joyful work culture where people are energized about being part of a great team and can have fun together.

A Joyful Work Culture

The effect of this joyful work culture goes beyond banking. It affects customers, their businesses, and how they live. Customers are at the heart of the way DBS does everything as it strives to develop remarkable solutions while building a more sustainable bank.

Internally, this joyful work culture drives psychological

Internally, this joyful work culture drives psychological safety and reinforces a high level of trust and collaboration among employees.

safety and reinforces a high level of trust and collaboration among employees. It takes the form of making decisions based on data and celebrating achievements.

ABCDE, MOJO, Joy Space, and PRIDE have been key initiatives in transforming the culture, so everyone has a shared passion in Making Banking Joyful.

CHAPTER 15

Adopting Agile

After visiting and studying how technology organizations operate, in 2016, bank leaders identified how intertwined business and technology were. They saw it as one domain, not as two separate domains.

To accelerate the fusion of these domains inside the bank, the leaders initiated agile platforms defined as "a set of applications with a set of people with a joint budget to deliver a joint strategy." But the term that more readily caught on across the whole bank as a mantra was "technology is business and business is technology."

Technology Is Business and Business Is Technology

This mantra led to creating platforms that merged the business and technology people. How? Tech and business employees were brought together by a shared strategy, objectives, and measures. In turn, they forced a shared dialogue around setting priorities (e.g., which one takes precedence: functionality versus stability?).

This approach, along with the Joy Space working environment, achieved something that many banks had been striving for over the years: removing the front-, middle-, and back-office mentality. It also contributed significantly to the bank's successful culture transformation.

> Tech and business employees were brought together by a shared strategy, objectives, and measures.

Two-in-a-Box Framework

Using a platform operating model brought technology and business together. It fused working relationships across internal teams that enabled faster decision-making, greater visibility, shared ownership, and dismantled silos. To enable this platform model, DBS implemented the two-in-a-box framework, also discussed in Best Practices in Chapter 7. It signaled how platforms were co-developed and maintained by the business and its technology partners working together on shared goals, business strategy, and an implementation road map.

In 2018, when the bank launched platforms as ecosystems, it saw a tremendous improvement in both the dialogue and relationship between business and technology. Since then, 33 distinct platforms have been generated around different businesses or vertical interests (e.g., data, payment, HR).

> In 2018, when the bank launched platforms as ecosystems, it saw a tremendous improvement in both the dialogue and relationship between business and technology.

To support the platform operating model, the bank set up a Platform Council of senior leaders who provide strategic support and guidance toward achieving objectives through platforms. Spurred by the mantra "technology is business and business is technology," they passionately believe that the platform operating model defines the future of business.

Moving to an Agile Platform

Teams in traditional organizations often move slowly, operate bureaucratically, lose sight of customer needs, and require too many meetings and layers of approvals. The agile methodology counters these challenges. To support the desired culture shift, those involved in initially adopting the agile methodology were moved around various teams across the bank.

Agile squads are small teams of about six people who have a clear objective to achieve in a short time. At least one team member is an expert or product owner in the area of the business being addressed. That person is charged with reinforcing the customer perspective throughout the process.

Today, when walking through the operations areas, it's common to see a team with members from different departments coming together for a 20-minute stand-up meeting to update everyone on its challenges and progress.

An early adopter of agile in the bank came from an unlikely area—the Audit Department.

Amazing Agile Audits

Imagine an environment in which the Audit team receives emails from business areas asking, "When will you audit us?" Now, you can start to grasp the success of the Audit team's transformation in leveraging agile. This team also receives thank-you notes after it completes an audit!

Auditing in the bank was transformed from a business *hindrance* to a business *enabler* in order to Make Banking Joyful. When you think of adopting agile, Audit is not the first area that naturally comes to mind, or even the second or third. And yet to understand the DBS transformation, it's important to understand the Audit Department's transformation and the larger role it played in bringing the benefits of digitalization to the bank.

Auditing in the bank was transformed from a business *hindrance* to a business *enabler* in order to Make Banking Joyful.

Audit is typically known as the "third line of defense." Business is the first line of defense, while corporate oversight functions (including Risk Management Group, and Group Legal and Compliance) make up the second line of defense. But the Audit team members challenged themselves by asking, "How can we play our role effectively in the Digital Wave?" To be successful, they knew they had to change—just as the rest of the bank was changing.

Before the Digital Wave, the Audit Department was perceived to be a policing function that limited information exchange within businesses. At times, auditors had to beg the business area for data. The approach was that the auditors scoped the audit based on the information on hand and their understanding of the business risks and level of controls. The decided-upon audit scope was then conveyed to the appropriate business. This process was relatively inflexible, scope-bound, time-consuming, and rigid due to the difficulty of responding to new scope requirements or late changes.

A breakthrough came in 2016 when the team was auditing T&O. The traditional audit methodology of being rigid, linear, and sequential could not deal with the regular agile sprints undertaken by T&O. Agile sprints were part of T&O's digitalization. Previously, new risks or unexpected areas of concern would not be easily factored into the audit scope; therefore, the team piloted a new auditing approach aimed at resolving the gaps and disconnects that could arise from traditional auditing methodology.

The new approach meant the team could participate in the Digital Wave by completely transforming the way its audit system worked. Team members were able to change the mindsets of those in their own team about how audits could be conducted differently. They then examined how to leverage data while being open to challenging the ways of conducting traditional audits. It wasn't just about AI, data mining, buying more systems, and using more applications. Rather, the change was about the *people* and the way they worked.

The Audit team used unbiased sample checking to identify threats based on certain roles representing the population. In effect, agile auditing technology moved the team from hindsight to insight. Specifically, it moved from:

- Past data samples to automated data download
- Manual data extraction and review to automated checks across the population
- Cyclical audits to on-demand auditing with continuous report generation

The team also questioned why it couldn't check 100 percent of the data and do one better—predict the areas with a higher likelihood of errors before they occurred. What started as this modest idea was applied in branches as risk profiling, and it had phenomenal consequences.

Branch Risk Profiling

In the Consumer bank, an early success came from using predictive analysis for its branch audits.

By leveraging machine learning techniques, the Audit team could predict which branches were likely to encounter risk events in the coming period. That led to allocating scarce resources and diving deeply into these branches as part of the audits.

Using a breadth of data (e.g., customer transactions and complaints, branch health, employee metrics, historical risk events), the team developed the Branch Risk Profiling (BRP) tool. This tool not only identified the potentially high-risk branches but also placed the spotlight on specific processes within a branch. In effect, it enabled the Audit team to achieve the best results when performing branch audits.

The benefits of using the Branch Risk Profiling (BRP) tool were quickly recognized by head office auditors in Singapore, where it was initiated. It is now used in most of the bank's major markets.

New Approach to Auditing

The Audit team's new approach for auditing required a fresh mindset across the bank. The pilot agile audit was based on the scrum approach developed by Jeff Sutherland and Ken Schwaber.[15]

---

15 "The Creators of Scrum, Ken Schwaber and Jeff Sutherland, Update the Scrum Guide," Scrum.org, November 17, 2017, https://www.scrum.org/resources/creators-scrum-ken-schwaber-and-jeff-sutherland-update-scrum-guide-0?gclid=Cj0KCQjwt4X8BRCPARIsABmcnOonjHBtTLZ2FD-cTSIw9fXuj31fn3y94d0_MSvW34XbpPKENZH6OGMaAp_6EALw_wcB.

In their agile way of managing a project, the work is left up to the team rather than management giving detailed instructions.

The pilot project succeeded. In 2017, just over 15 percent (28 of the audits in the bank) agile audits were conducted, a number that rose to 50 percent (93 audits) in 2018. Initially, two members of the Audit team were trained to be scrum masters, and now there are over 40.

To draw a comparison, the old audit methodology was a six- to eight-week intervention with little collaboration from the business. The audit itself was time-consuming and a lot of work. Agile audits today dramatically reduce any interruption to the business due to much of the work being done independently by the Audit team. Meetings with business heads no longer consist of days locked in a conference room. Instead, those involved hold 20-minute meetings called "Sprints" in their offices.

Sprint Zero Workshops to Identify Risk Points

An agile audit starts with a Sprint Zero workshop. Its purpose is to share an overview of the new approach, and features a half-day, end-to-end process walkthrough with the business being audited. It includes participants role-playing to develop their skills of discussing an audit with a business head.

Sprint Zero involves both the Audit team and the Business team jointly identifying key risk and control points. Yes, the business helps identify where fraud might be happening!

Together, the teams identify risk points in Sprints, which are short sessions held over two weeks. The whole process—from planning to final report—takes six to eight weeks. But instead of pulling the people from the business out from their work for long periods, the Audit team works together with the businesspeople for short intervals. That's why the meetings are called Sprints.

Besides transforming the approach, the audits are also an example of transforming communication, with the Audit team communicating with Business heads in the role of trusted advisors.

Tooling Up: Sprint, Kanban Board, Timebox, MoSCoW

The Business and the Audit teams collaborate in the Sprint process to identify risk points. But this approach seems to defy the logic of an audit. Why warn potential suspects that the areas they may have committed fraud in are about to be audited? The Audit team has a sixth sense. Using audit tools, team members pick up on both peoples' reaction in the Sprint as well as the analyses. From these, they can identify warning signals.

To ensure the audit runs smoothly and on time, they use Kanban boards—visual whiteboards used in the agile approach to show workflow. If the name sounds familiar, it's because Kanban boards have been adopted from quality improvement initiatives. The Kanban boards are viewable by everyone in the audit, thus making the risks transparent to all stakeholders. That way, no surprises emerge in the audit, as both the Business and the Audit team contribute to the board. An essential benefit is that the audit gets broken down into bite-size, manageable components. Using the board also builds trust in the audit and assists in identifying the Sprints.

The Sprints break down the audit into "Timeboxed" durations.

Timebox is a core tool used by agile audit. Using it, participants agree to strict time boundaries around an action and individual deliverables of the team members. They decide that the meeting will last only, say, 30 minutes and then state what the deliverables from the meeting will be. By default, having Timebox forces presenters to prioritize what's most important.

During agile audits, Timebox also shows the time required for the audit and keeps it running on schedule. This tool reinforces to everyone that the audit won't become a hindrance by consuming too much time—a common complaint of the old auditing approach.

Timeboxing focuses the team on the task at hand and drives productivity as members deliver smaller actions in shorter deadlines. Also, the individuals involved don't want to be listed on the Kanban board as being responsible for slowing down the audit.

Employees have a tendency to allow their work to expand to the time available—a practice so common, it even has its own name: Parkinson's Law. Timebox overcomes this tendency and keeps people on track.

Another tool adopted from the agile approach is called "MoSCoW." MoSCoW enables both the Business and the Audit team to agree on which actions are a Must (M), Should (S), Could (C), or Won't (W) in applying the risk points. This tool prioritizes what needs to be done and what should *not* be done, an equally important judgment.

Also used in agile auditing is the Issue Register—a record of all issues within the audit. It assists in the periodization and monitoring of issues, and tracks the success of the actions being taken. It also assists in minimizing an issue's impact.

Award-Winning Approach

The Audit Department at DBS has been recognized for its innovative approach, but surprisingly not by a banking association. Its engineering achievement has been singled out by the

Institute of Engineers in Singapore. In 2015 and 2016, this association gave the Audit team its Achievement Award for technology innovation.

Also, in 2016, the team received the ASEAN Outstanding Engineering Achievement Award for its role in developing a data analytics-driven solution for detecting and preventing trading irregularities in Singapore. This came from the ASEAN Federation of Engineering Organizations.

Auditing Treasury Department

One place the agile audit was especially well received was in the Treasury Department, where time is literally money. The Sprints and overall effectiveness of the new auditing approach minimized the Treasury team's time away from managing the bank's money.

Auditing AI

The Audit team is now addressing how to audit the AI being adopted across the bank. As the bank grows and implements more systems with a greater exchange of data, the need to track performance increases. For example, how does the team audit a chatbot? What new algorithm is needed to audit the current algorithm?

Today, the Audit team is able to conduct more audits faster with no additional crew members. It has learned to work more efficiently while it leverages predictive auditing and analyzes the data.

Agile audit represented the type of new thinking and approach the bank was looking for. It fitted perfectly into Making Banking Joyful and, just as important, it made auditing joyful for the employees! This agile audit story encapsulates DBS's transformation success and the bank's openness to being a learning organization.

CHAPTER 16

Be a Learning Organization

DBS believed that building a growth mindset among its employees was critical so they could continuously learn, grow, and adapt. This belief translated into continual innovation, growth, and resilience across the organization while building individual career resilience.

To have new and effective ways of learning, the bank created experiential learning programs such as hackathons. This is where employees worked with start-ups, leading organizations, and coders to experiment with solutions that addressed big-business challenges. Initiatives were also installed that empowered bank employees to own their own reskilling and upskilling.

Here are 10 best practices the bank employed to become a better learning organization.

Best Practices to Become a Learning Organization

Best Practices #1: No Manager's Approval Requirement for Training

Early on, a decision was made to eliminate a manager's approval for taking a training course that cost less than $500 as a way to empower employees to upgrade their skills. This resulted in a higher engagement and learning by employees while encouraging them to have an individual growth mindset.

Early on, a decision was made to eliminate a manager's approval for taking a training course that cost less than $500 as a way to empower employees to upgrade their skills.

There was one condition, though. After taking the training, every employee had to teach colleagues what he or she learned. This practice enhanced the bank's learning culture, supported employees in learning new skills and worked as a natural peer pressure controller, as employees did not want to embarrass themselves in front of their colleagues. Today, an employee at DBS can select from over 6,000 different courses.

Best Practices #2: Back to School

Implementing the Digital Wave meant reinventing the bank. For employees, that translated into a need to learn new jobs, which required a culture of learning.

The result was a Back to School initiative. Inspired by Google's "g2g" (Googler-to-Googler) teaching network, employees dedicate a portion of their time to helping their peers learn important skills.

Back to School programs featured masterclasses taught mostly by internal subject-matter experts in a school-like environment. Teachers included GANDALF scholars who first learned and then taught their colleagues about the required technology architecture.

Since its launch in 2017, Back to School has led to the creation of more than 100 teachers. By 2020, it had more than 9,000 participants and 11,000 views of its bite-sized videos.

Best Practices #3: Learn By Doing

Learning makes up only 10 percent of a person's transformation; *doing* makes up the rest.

The term "Learn by Doing" was adopted early in the Digital Wave implementation after it became clear that teaching people to be technology literate in a classroom didn't work.

Learn by Doing was initially driven by the Transformation team, which encouraged employees to participate in customer journeys, design thinking, agile, hackathons, and other activities. The bank focused on creating an environment in which it was safe to experiment and fail. It even gave awards for failing and for daring to ask for money.

Learning makes up only 10 percent of a person's transformation; *doing* makes up the rest.

Best Practices #4: Adopting Hackathons

Introduced into the bank in 2015, hackathons have supported the belief that people learn from doing. They help build transformation success by providing a platform for employees to do just that. Employees could observe what was possible when they applied digitalization and saw how quickly new solutions could be created and implemented.

The early hackathons built momentum, especially the first hackathon that led to the creation of Digibank. Some of the participants from the first hackathon say it was a defining moment in their careers.

DBS's approach to hackathons is that participants start by discussing digitalization and trends. Then they include start-up entrepreneurs from outside the bank as participants and spend the two days resolving a business problem. During those two days, bankers and entrepreneurs address issues by leveraging each other's strengths as they collaboratively seek a technology solution.

Hackathons have also been tremendously successful in challenging leaders' beliefs that these types of solutions required six months and millions of dollars to develop.

Best Practices #5: Over-40 Hackathon

In the third hackathon the bank ever conducted, Piyush had only one rule: *all DBS people on the teams had to be over age 40.* This over-40 hackathon was conducted to eliminate the belief that digitalization was only for younger employees—that older employees could not keep up. Once this was proven wrong, people started to believe in the older generation's ability to change.

This was a shrewd move considering that many organizations struggle with the mindset that older employees cannot adopt

In the third hackathon the bank ever conducted, Piyush had only one rule: *all DBS people on the teams had to be over age 40.*

digitalization. It also reinforced Piyush's desire to "make his sheep wolves," as mentioned in Chapter 7.

Best Practices #6: DBS Global Hackathon – A Paradigm Shift

In 2019, DBS invited more than 1,000 participants from 67 countries to compete for a total prize of US$100,000. This hackathon aimed to use a customer-centric approach to developing cutting-edge services through ideation, prototyping, and pitching to the bank. It was looking for innovative, future-forward solutions. Featured themes were hyper-personalization, everyday insurance, AI in retail banking, and sustainability, among other topics.

More than 300 teams worked with 74 mentors from the bank and its partners. Over the span of 17 weeks, they developed a working prototype that leveraged machine learning, augmented reality, virtual reality, IoT, and more to improve customer experiences. Teams from Russia, Indonesia, Malaysia, and Singapore made the final selection.

At the end of the final 48-hour sprint, "We Shift Paradigm"—a team of three from Malaysia—edged out 11 other teams with its idea of building a more inclusive banking system.

Best Practices #7: Pre-Incubator to Work

In another approach, the bank set up a pre-incubator to work with start-ups predominantly outside of Fintech. At DBS, these pre-incubator projects are not investments; they are developmental opportunities.

Pre-incubator was a three-month program that provided facilities, mentoring, and access to about 15 start-up companies.

For example, one start-up was making bamboo bikes; another was researching how to use the ugly fruit that supermarkets did not want.

The pre-incubator approach also allowed exposure to leaders to participate with the start-ups by mentoring teams or being in attendance when they pitched. This approach has evolved and given birth to successes such as JIM, the HR chatbot, food delivery (via Facebook messenger), and many more solutions.

Best Practices #8: Wreckoon – Challenging the Status Quo

Wreckoon is the DBS learning organization's mascot. This self-service tool operated by always pushing boundaries to test the best ideas and assumptions.

Taking a leaf out of the Netflix Chaos Engineering playbook and building on it, DBS created Wreckoon as a self-service tool to test the resilience of applications in development. Using Wreckoon is a compulsory requirement in every meeting and presentation deck.

Taking a leaf out of the Netflix Chaos Engineering playbook and building on it, DBS created Wreckoon as a self-service tool to test the resilience of applications in development.

As a visual, the bank created an image of a raccoon with a hammer and at its feet a pile of rocks saying "status quo." This image appeared in meetings as a reminder to challenge the status quo by pausing and encouraging different views. The image also included the copy, "P.S. What would Wreckoon say?" Six thought-provoking questions followed:

1. What is our riskiest assumption?
2. What are the trade-offs?
3. What could go wrong?
4. Where is the data?
5. What is our weakest link?
6. What have we missed out on?

At the bottom of the image, the P.S. stated, "Psychological safety is about creating a safe environment for everyone to speak up and encourage differentiating views."

Best Practices #9: Adopting Artificial Intelligence and Machine Learning

To futureproof its employees, bank leaders collaborated with Amazon Web Services (AWS) to develop a critical mass of employees equipped with fundamental skills in Artificial Intelligence (AI) and Machine Learning (ML). The aim was to accelerate the use of AI and ML across the bank.

DBS and AWS jointly launched the DBS x AWS DeepRacer League. DBS employees learned the basics of AI and ML by participating in a series of hands-on online tutorials. Next, they put their new knowledge to the test by programming their own autonomous model race car. These ML models were then uploaded onto a virtual racing environment. There, employees experimented and fine-tuned their models as they engaged in friendly competition.

About 3,000 employees, including the bank's senior leadership, have participated in the DBS x AWS DeepRacer League. It has complemented the bank's effort to scale up its digital learning tools and platforms, which enable employees to upgrade their skills and pick up new knowledge—even when they are not physically in the office.

Best Practices #10: Reskilling Employees

By 2016, bank leaders had identified about 1,200 jobs (e.g., bank tellers, contact center people, etc.) that would disappear over the next few years. They started an active rescaling program that created a whole skills matrix for individual jobs. Specifically, they identified which current jobs could be translated into future jobs and what skills would be required.

In 2020, bank leaders again identified jobs that were going to disappear. They realized that 3,000 people would be affected, and they're actively working to rescale them for alternative jobs.

Also, to support the rescaling of employees, in 2017, the bank invested $20 million over five years in a program to develop its workforce to function well in a digital world. This program encouraged large-scale participation and digital adoption by all employees. It involved:

- AI-powered e-learning that could be accessed 24/7
- Experiential learning, such as intrapreneur programs and hackathons; this allowed employees to go on paid sabbaticals, work on prototypes, and start their own businesses
- Grants and scholarships in the form of a $1,000 investment for individual training
- Innovative learning spaces including the DBS Academy and DBS Asia X (innovation hub)

Part of this effort included the launch of DigiFY in 2017. This was a mobile learning platform and online course intended to transform key employees into digital bankers. DigiFY imparted skills in seven categories: agile, data-driven, digital business models, digital communications, digital technologies, journey thinking, and risk and controls. Once employees achieve mastery in a three-part course, they are qualified to teach those precepts to their coworkers. More than 80 percent of DBS's employees have been through the curriculum.

Another part of this effort was the introduction of Data Heroes, a program to build data analytics capabilities. Data Heroes is a six-month program with an intensive and hands-on curriculum to equip employees with the skills and mindset of a data translator.

The bank also encourages experiential learning and experimentations through its DBS Xplore program in which employees stretch themselves by participating in cross-departmental projects. All the learning was conducted while reminding employees to remain customer obsessed.

CHAPTER 17

Customer Obsessed

Being customer obsessed is not simply a slogan at DBS bank; it's embedded into its DNA. Everyday operations and efforts to resolve challenges start by thinking about the "job to be done" for the customer and employs customer journeys to find new solutions.

One management school of thought is that if you look after your employees, they will look after your customers, who will then assure your financial performance. In DBS, the philosophy is to first look after the customers, and doing so will look after the employees. In combination, they will take care of the financials.

Being customer obsessed is not simply a slogan at DBS bank; it's embedded into its DNA.

Being customer obsessed is included in the third strategic principle as a reinforcement of how important serving the customer is throughout the

In DBS, the philosophy is to first look after the customers, and doing so will look after the employees.

organization. Consider two examples from the Consumer bank and Human Resources.

Example One: Consumer Bank Becomes More Customer Obsessed

The Consumer bank is the most publicly visual part of DBS, which makes its part of the digital transformation the most noticeable of all.

To guide the implementation of Making Banking Joyful, the Consumer team identified these three core principles to become more customer obsessed:

1. Product design had to be customer centric by using design thinking.
2. Customer journey had to be designed for no calls, no branches, and no cash.
3. The STP (Straight-Through Processing) Mount Everest Challenge had to be conquered.

1. Product design had to be customer centric by using design thinking.

Every product group and channel had to embrace these principles and reinvent the way team members thought about their products and services and how they delivered them to customers. The 4Ds framework was identified as the tool to aid in this transformation while enabling the group to leverage design thinking.

2. Customer journey had to be designed for no calls, no branches, and no cash.

The Consumer bank team sought to transform by operating without branches. This meant enabling a simple, easy, seamless online journey that would drive customers' behavior shifts to the internet and/or smartphones. This, in turn, involved driving consumer behavior toward no calls to the call center, and leveraging online services for financial transactions and digital payments, thus removing the need for cash.

The bank recognizes a segment of customers who still want to visit a branch. For example, some customers use the physical "POSB Passbook" that can be updated at the ATM. (POSB Bank was acquired by DBS in 1998.) The "no call, no branch, no cash" experience is a core design principle.

3. The STP (Straight-Through Processing) Mount Everest Challenge had to be conquered.

Banks have been notorious for building walls between divisions (e.g., Consumer versus Corporate) and then building more walls between departments within their own division. The term "front-, middle-, and back-office" was once common language in banking. But in a digitally driven bank, this term not only ceases to exist, but it *can't* exist. The business has to move as one in the same direction, requiring teams across different departments to collaborate in an agile culture.

The business has to move as one in the same direction, requiring teams across different departments to collaborate in an agile culture.

The Digital Wave initiatives provided the structure and opportunity for the Consumer bank to transform how it was operating. Leaders focused on moving toward "no operations," which meant automating everything, also called STP (straight-through processing).

STP is another Mount Everest challenge within banking, as it eliminates the opportunity of human error, improves customer service, and is less cost intensive. In the past, initiatives such as Six Sigma were adopted to conquer the STP Mount Everest Challenge. Certain initiatives made what was considered to be significant inroads at the time. Today, they pale in importance to the success of transforming into a digitally driven bank.

Example Two: HR Becomes Internally Customer Obsessed

Being customer obsessed is not only about *external* customers; it's also about *internal* customers. In implementing Making Banking Joyful, the HR Department went through its own digital transformation driven by these three pillars:

> Being customer obsessed is not only about *external* customers; it's also about *internal* customers.

- Be customer obsessed and create amazing products and experiences.
- Digitize HR by automating the entire employee life cycle and leveraging RPA (Robotics Process Automation), AI (Artificial Intelligence), and chatbots.
- Be data driven and make decisions powered by data and insights.

These three pillars cut across the candidate and employee life cycles in how the bank attracts, retains, and engages talent. Key outcomes included increasing operational efficiency, optimizing resources, mitigating risk, and creating joyful candidate and employee experiences.

As part of the bank's transformation, the HR team built its own Human Capital Analytics (HCA). The HCA team addresses the entire spectrum of people analytics—from reporting to predictive modeling—while providing insights on hiring, retention, and productivity.

As part of the bank's transformation, the HR team built its own Human Capital Analytics (HCA).

The HR team also led the way in upskilling the workforce by continually introducing new platforms on the employee value proposition. Today, platforms are being introduced in various ways—from writing algorithms that predict resignations to creating AI recruiters and conducting internal customer journeys.

After a comprehensive review of employee benefits that integrated employee feedback and market benchmarking, in 2018, HR rolled out several enhancements. Changes included:

- "iFlex$" – a flexible spending benefit
- "iHealth" – a portal for information around health and wellness
- Dependents' protection insurance – to help defray living expenses in raising surviving child(ren) of employees who pass on while in service to the bank

As employee expectations and the nature of work evolves, DBS's HR team continues to redesign the culture to make people's lives better. The goal is to balance the financial with the nonfinancial benefits as the whole bank focuses on being more data driven—and more joyful.

CHAPTER 18

Data-Driven Culture

A key component from the start of the Digital Wave implementation was to identify how the bank could use data to scale the digital experience to the level of the other members of GANDALF (Google, Amazon, Netflix, DBS, Apple, LinkedIn, and Facebook) and to leverage data to improve the number and frequency of "wow" reactions from customers.

Making Banking Joyful meant being agile, highly efficient, and constantly on the edge of innovation with the ability to scale and perform extremely well. It also required being data driven.

Measuring whether an application's rating is up or down is *not* an indicator for Making Banking Joyful. Where data overlaps with customers is where the magic happens. Performance is now measured across the bank in the 99th percentile, with data

Making Banking Joyful meant being agile, highly efficient, and constantly on the edge of innovation with the ability to scale and perform extremely well.

being transformed to drive the high performance required to deliver the Digital Wave.

> Where data overlaps with customers is where the magic happens.

The organization's overriding theme in transforming to a data-driven culture was to maximize value using data for the customer, for determining risk (both credit and operational), and for revenue. This happened because of employees adopting data in their day-to-day decision-making and by targeting a handful of large, infrequent initiatives in which the bank could realize exponential results.

Data Driven Operating Model (DDOM)

The bank used the term Data Driven Operating Model (DDOM) as the acronym that explained the restructuring to data-driven culture. DDOM is evolving within the bank especially as the use of AI increases.

Initially, though, the transformation to a data-driven culture started with these three pillars:

1. **Building the Culture and Capability** – Build the skills and culture across the bank while creating data scientists, stewards, and champions to drive value creation.
2. **Enabling Data Usage** – Make data frictionless to get access to quality data while maintaining control.
3. **Building a Fit-for-Purpose Data Platform** – Build a scalable, secure, cost-effective architecture and tool set, then populate it with data-driven use cases.

1. Building the Culture and Capability

Creating a data-driven culture was more about transforming the behaviors of the bank employees than about the data itself. The analytics were the easy part; the hard part was encouraging people to change their working approach. For example, initially, people were being protective of their own data and reluctant to share it. This had to change. The bank worked on developing automatic access (no approval required) to data. The access to data depended on each individual's level in the bank and how the data would be used.

Creating a data-driven culture was more about transforming the behaviors of the bank employees than about the data itself.

To transform every employee in every business in every country to a data-driven culture was an ambitious goal. The Transformation team (the Data office reports to the Transformation office) wanted to create small successes to build confidence in this new strategic and digital way of working. The more the bank could enable people, the more they would use the data. Two of the initial successes included:

- **Better Data, Better Decisions**

For years, the bank was already using big data and focusing on analytics. In 2014, it had partnered with the Singapore Agency for Science, Technology and Research to create its own lab and have its data scientists work with the bankers. Anyone in the bank who came up with a good idea was supported by being given access to the lab and the opportunity to experiment. The aim was to make participating in data analytics fun. So once a quarter, people bid with their ideas. Those selected would go off and "play" at the lab.

This non-threatening approach encouraged people to learn about what data analytics could do, especially early on in the adoption of big data when few people understood its potential value. This laid the groundwork for the Analytics team.

- **Cross-Sell to Cross-Buy Solution Gleaned from the Data**

In banking, a key opportunity is cross-selling products to customers. With the cost of customer acquisition being high, cross-selling means once you become a customer, the bank aims to sell you more products and services.

When banks use data to understand their customers better and the context in which they operate, this allows them to make recommendations. Employees ask, "Given the data gleaned, what would attract a customer to cross-buy a product?"

Shifting from cross-selling to cross-buying was aided by using the data available, but it took considerable effort and time to get to that point.

2. Enabling Data Usage

The Transformation team's focus was to encourage everyone in the bank to become comfortable using data analytics, whether small or large, basic analytics or machine learning. Team members set the initial goal of having 200 data-driven initiatives across the bank. Examples were predicting mortgage customer

The Transformation team's focus was to encourage everyone in the bank to become comfortable using data analytics, whether small or large, basic analytics or machine learning.

attrition, predicting which customer would call the customer service center, and reducing false positives for AML (anti-money laundering).

> "With global trade set to grow and increased regulatory demands on anti-money-laundering and fraud prevention, we believe in taking a proactive approach in enhancing our current risk management processes. Our trade alerts program has helped the bank create a more robust platform to detect trade anomalies. The bank is now able to use big data to manage the overall transactional trends more effectively." – *Yang Ping (MD, Technology and Operations)*[16]

Another initial challenge was to move data reporting from a static report to real-time decision-making. This was not easy for an organization used to reporting and presenting historical data using slide decks. To start with, Transformation team members asked the business heads, "What decision are you aiming to make?" Then by using design thinking, they worked on the data visualization each business needed to make better decisions. From existing reports, they could also see what decisions users were making. Once the key decisions were clarified and agreed upon, the designers then worked to build a dashboard prototype that highlighted those decisions and the relevant insights required. This led to a prototype that was tested and then finalized.

This approach transformed the business by thinking about the problem to solve and not the data to use—an important distinction.

Some of the success in enabling data usage included:

16 "DBS leverages big data analytics to reduce trade anomalies," DBS.com, accessed April 15, 2021, https://www.dbs.com/newsroom/DBS_leverages_big_data_analytics_to_reduce_trade_anomalies.

- **Reducing the Number of Reports**

The Analytics team reviewed the number of monthly reports sent out across the bank. The team then conducted an exercise: It stopped sending all reports and waited to see who asked for them! Next, it eliminated the reports that weren't being requested. Through workshops, the Analytics team went on to train employees to extract data themselves and to create only the reports they needed.

It stopped sending all reports and waited to see who asked for them!

In another example, HR was spending time creating several reports a month. The Analytics team worked with the HR team to reduce that number. Not happy with the initial reduction, it also made the decision not to send any reports *at all* the following month. Only 20 requests were received, and the reports not requested were eliminated. Today, all HR guidelines and policies are available online with the plan to become a paperless office.

- **Predicting RM Departures**

Another early success was using predictive analytics and modeling to identify when an RM (Relationship Manager) was considering leaving the bank. In many banks, RM turnover is high. At the time, the data was just sitting in the bank not being used. Members of the Analytics team and HR discovered that certain data would allow them to predict if RMs were likely to leave. The data included:

- Their first sick day and how quickly they took it
- Their number of days training
- Their branch's location

- Their monthly revenue
- Their leave patterns

The 600 data points of the common/respective behaviors that employees demonstrated before they resigned were fed into the machine learning. With 85 percent accuracy, it told the bank which people were likely to leave within three months.

Today, this model creates a monthly report (a digital nudge) that alerts supervisors about potential employees resigning, and it prescribes specific actions managers can take. When they take these corrective actions, the bank retains more than 90 percent of employees who might ordinarily have left. And for every 1 percent improvement in reducing turnover, the bank can save up to $5 million.

As these successes became known across the bank, leaders in other departments examined how they could also use data analytics productively. Here are more examples:

- **Creating Exponential Results**

As data analytics has evolved within the bank, its leaders have become savvier at creating exponential results from the data. For example, studying the data can help predict failures in apps before they happen or solve customers' queries in the call center before they even know they have them.

The bank now uses data to understand its customers better and applies that to:

- Engage customers in a more contextual manner
- Service customers in a more contextual manner including predictive analytics
- Identify and rectify any failures customers are having

- Reward customers with surprises such as for being a long-term customer

The Analytics team rolled out algorithms to solve questions such as which credit card offers are most relevant in each market and when. It also focused on using Customer Science to predict customer issues and eliminate them before customers became aware of them. For example, the team tracked every interaction from the customer bank app internally and watched how customers used it. "What was their behavior? When did they drop off, log on and off, etc.?" Studying this data resulted in consolidating it for the business and using it to leverage the time series forecasting modeling called Prophet[17] to identify possible future failures.

The Analytics team also created a center of excellence with two groups of people—data scientists and translators. These groups worked with business heads to maximize the value of the data.

- **Data Analytics for Anti-Money Laundering (AML)**

Data analytics is particularly effective in AML, an area in which the percentage of false positives can be as high as 98 percent. A false positive is a result that wrongly indicates a particular condition is present.

Every time the system delivered an alert, the situation had to be investigated. So, the Analytics team adopted machine learning to review the false positives flagged by the system. As

17 Prophet is a Facebook open sourcing forecasting tool available in Python and R. It is fast and provides completely automated forecasts that can be turned by hand by data scientists and analysts. For more information, visit https://facebook.github.io/prophet.

the machine learned the rule of AML, the number of false positives were reduced, thus freeing up time to focus on real cases.

- **Skills for Machine Learning**

As people in the bank experimented with the analytics, their skills and decision-making improved. They could also define problems better as specific parameters were required. This is especially relevant for machine learning because users need to clearly stipulate the problem. If they don't, then they won't know what they want to solve and neither does the machine.

- **Data Everywhere**

Employees realized that they always had some data available to get started and could acquire additional data later. The message was, "Don't let having limited data be an excuse for not proceeding with data analytics."

The Analytics team encouraged employees to use simple analytics tools at least every three months and to implement the output of the analysis. It emphasized that not all analyses needed complex/advanced tools. In most cases, they could start with using tools such as Microsoft Excel, Python, and QlikView. Employees across the bank could try tools on a small scale, see what worked, and identify what needed to change. This would build momentum and traction, which leads to early successes.

"Don't let having limited data be an excuse for not proceeding with data analytics."

- **Dashboard Culture**

Some of the biggest traction happened in 2017 with the bank's move to a dashboard culture. Reporting was then driven by

Some of the biggest traction happened in 2017 with the bank's move to a dashboard culture.

automated dashboards. Why was this better? Because bank leaders wanted to only see consistently designed dashboards in their decision-making meetings rather than slide decks. The goal was to translate data visualization into easy-to-understand dashboards that enabled employees to be more productive and make better decisions.

In addition, creating automated dashboards eliminated significant effort in generating reports. And dashboarding *everything* as a way of conducting business kept the message "this organization does things differently" top of mind for everybody.

- **Design for Data**

The Analytics team worked simultaneously on small and large data-driven challenges, knowing many of the large ones would take a few years to implement. It continued to adopt continuous improvement and learning while scaling data first. It also ensured that data-driven analytics became operationalized and machine learning became part of the process that resulted in maximum value.

Today, the bank recognizes the need to combine machine learning and advanced analytics with human intuition to maximize results.

The team also looked at how to build in "Design for Data" as a fundamental across the bank. This meant, for example, that every time designers built a new feature or app, they were required to think of the data up front rather than after the app had gone live. Team members never wanted to say later, "We wish we'd had that data."

Today, the bank recognizes the need to combine machine learning and advanced analytics with human intuition to maximize results. It also uses data and digital dashboards to map every step of its customers' journeys. This helps prevent issues from arising and keeps customers engaged profitably, thus allowing the bank to increase its "share of wallet."

- **Increased Share of Wallet**

The beauty of the digital lens is the ability to delve deep into the data and, as a result, make better decisions. The data allows leaders to confirm any hypotheses they made on revenue and profit gains.

At the start of the digital journey, the bank set up its databases and data warehouses to start tracking what the digital transformation meant in terms of stakeholder value creation. From seeing the degree of digital activity, leaders could track the increase in their revenues, reduction in costs, and therefore the improvement in return on equity.

By studying the data over time, leaders concluded that when a customer converted from traditional to digital, the bank's revenue grew faster. Also, when a customer stays digital, that person's revenue grows faster than the person who stays traditional or reverts to traditional from digital.

For the data to be reliable, leaders also needed to ensure it was not influenced by special factors. For example, "Was there a large cohort of its wealthiest customers that converted from traditional to digital?" If yes, this would have created a need to study the data over time to ensure the hypothesis held. In fact, results revealed that it was a causation effect rather than correlation, which meant when customers became digital, they would do more activities with the bank, thus contributing to higher revenues and greater profits.

Customer data also allowed the bank to understand which customers to encourage to become digital and which needed both digital and traditional channels. For example, while the top end of private banking customers may adopt digital channels, they could still heavily rely on advice from their RMs to make decisions.

Today, the bank is focused on hyper-personalization by strengthening its data analysis and artificial intelligence (AI) capabilities.

3. Building a Fit-for-Purpose Data Platform

The bank created data platforms to transform it into a data-led organization that delivered intuitive products and services, including:

- **Robotic Process Automation (RPA)**

At the end of 2017, the bank partnered with IBM to create a center of excellence using RPA. The intent was to optimize numerous business processes across the bank.

- **Chatbot – HiRi**

In 2018, the HR Department launched "HiRi," an AI-powered employee chatbot that provides easy, instant, and personalized responses to HR matters 24/7. This self-service chatbot alleviates routine transactions such as employees calling to check on the number of days leave they have left. This also allows HR personnel to focus on more strategic interactions.

- **JIM – AI Recruiter**

One of the most successful experiments and use of data has been JIM, short for Jobs Intelligence Maestro. In 2018, the bank launched Southeast Asia's first virtual recruitment bot to make hiring wealth planning managers more efficient.

One of the most successful experiments and use of data has been JIM, short for Jobs Intelligence Maestro.

In that year the bank hired 40 percent more wealth planning managers to support its rapidly growing wealth management business. With the increased number of applicants, recruiters were spending up to 20 percent of their time collecting information and responding to emails before meeting with their shortlisted candidates. The HR team sought ways to simplify the process. The bank also wanted to mitigate the risk of bias from, for example, cultural backgrounds, schools attended, or grade point averages alone. A key impetus was also to make the journey "joyful" for recruiters and candidates.

JIM automated the prescreening process of reviewing résumés, collecting applicants' responses for interview questions, and conducting psychometric assessments.

DBS collaborated with a start-up called "impress.ai." Working through the challenges and overcoming security concerns in sharing information with this four-person start-up took 12 months. The HR team acquired new skills in the process. Many in HR can call themselves chatbot coaches.

Today, JIM reviews résumés, collects applicants' responses for pre-screening questions, conducts psychometric profiling assessments, and answers questions. Its benefits are numerous:

- 24/7 – Candidates can apply to join DBS at any time of any day; they don't need to take time off of work. The process is less painful for the candidate, and internally, recruiters save around 40 man-hours a month.
- Removes bias – Candidates are able to check online what the bank is about, its culture and environment. They can view a video job description and ask JIM questions. If they like what they see, they can then move on to part two.
- Screening – Leveraging data analytics, the bank has built a profile of a top sales performer. This information informs the way HR assesses candidates. For example, candidates might answer situational questions that demonstrate their ability to manage difficult customers.
- Psychometric Test – Candidates have the flexibility to take the psychometric test at a time that works best for them. Prior to JIM, the dropout rate at this stage was 50 percent for reasons such as candidates not having time to test in person or recruiters not following through.

Once candidates complete the test successfully, they are invited to schedule an interview.

In addition, a new hire's probation period was changed from three to six months to give the person time to build sales numbers. As the modeling revealed, three months was simply too short a time to see results. Because of JIM and these changes, the bank's churn rate of sales new hires dropped from 27 to 18 percent.

- **Quantum Image Recognition Application – QIRA**

QIRA is a workforce command center bot developed by the bank to monitor and send alerts on call queues at busy customer centers. Implementing QIRA—from its initial kick-off to "go-live"—happened within six months.

QIRA optimized resources in real time by leveraging RPA to transform the current command center mode through digitalization and automation. It led to more efficient management and distribution of workloads, which resulted in a six-time increase of load-balancing speed. This improvement allowed employees to focus more time on value-added tasks, such as analyzing real-time trends and proposed customer improvements.

- **Data Lake ADA/ALAN**

DBS's AI protocol (called ALAN) aimed to establish a standardized protocol to:

- Enable a common way of working that supports iterative improvement
- Encourage the creation of reusable assets

ALAN reinforced best practices across the bank and improved the tracking and control of risks using various tools.

- **Control Tower**

The Control Tower was launched to monitor customer journeys in real time. This meant setting up an airport-style Control Tower with only a handful of people in it who ran the total technology activity of the bank.

They oversee everything, only needing to manage exceptions in real time. The team explained the need for real time by leveraging the airport-style Control Tower, "There is no

The Control Tower was launched to monitor customer journeys in real time.

point reconciling debris on the runway today from a request yesterday."

Some team members in the Control Tower are managing in real time, driven by data and dealing with exceptions across Operations. Others in the Control Tower are supporting the business to grow, analyzing data to improve customer journeys, and overseeing and managing risk and control. This represents business as usual. Today, the team calls its meetings (no surprise) Control Tower meetings.

In Control Tower meetings, employees discuss the tracking and progress of a number of key themes that include:

- Demand and workforce management
- Customer journeys and behavior
- Life experimentation and campaigns
- Health of the system including smart notifications and alerts
- Issue prevention

The Control Tower's value is to provide enhanced customer profitability and to move toward employees being more joyful at work. It also provides optimization of campaigns, "golden path" adherence, preemptive issue resolution, workforce automation, real-time insights, and a competitive edge in doing business.

Today, the bank has built a unified and scalable data platform that has more than 400 analytics users, an analytics sandbox, and a data factory that accelerates value-based ingestion. About 60 percent of relevant data is now accessible from a single source. It uses predictive technology to ensure it has the right offerings to customers at the right time and digitally nudges them toward a specific action.

The bank has also developed an analytic center of excellence. It has more than 150 advanced analytics initiatives and over 18,000 employees. That includes more than 1,000 leaders trained on using data and over 1,400 data heroes acting as data translators.

CHAPTER 19

Experiment and Take Risks

In traditional banking, the idea is to mitigate risk. But as part of DBS's transformation and any digital transformation, its leaders wanted to *encourage* risk—to behave like a start-up and be open to experimentation. Employees who typically want to protect their jobs and their bonuses have learned to play safe—the opposite of what was required for DBS to implement the Digital Wave.

But as part of DBS's transformation and any digital transformation, its leaders wanted to *encourage* risk—to behave like a start-up and be open to experimentation.

To encourage employees to experiment and take risks, the following approaches were taken.

1. Create a Safe Environment to Experiment

In creating a culture that encouraged risk-taking and failure, the leaders had to lead by example and set the right expectations. They started by *not* holding employees accountable for every last piece of success. This encouraged people to participate in changes at any level and be recognized for trying. It also unlocked their energy, creativity, and imagination. This proved particularly effective in areas such as customer journey and data transformation.

The leaders also recognized how fear of failure could impede innovation and realized that some experiments needed to fail before success could happen.

> They started by *not* holding employees accountable for every last piece of success.

To eliminate the fear of failure and create a safe environment to experiment in, the bank based its approach on the concept of psychological safety. The concept of psychological safety[18] has been developed by Amy Edmondson, Novartis Professor of Leadership and Management at Harvard Business School.

DBS leaders became passionate about creating a safe environment for everyone to experiment, as these examples of successful change show:

- **Changing Customers' Call Center Habit**

An interesting experiment in the call center was to encourage customers to move to online digital solutions rather than calling the bank. This experiment started by playing this message for

18 "Creating Psychological Safety in the Workplace," HBS. org, January 22, 2019, https://hbr.org/ideacast/2019/01/creating-psychological-safety-in-the-workplace.

customers who called: "If you would like a faster digital way to complete your inquiry, please press one." When they did, they were given the bank's website. Having a high volume of calls redirected digitally made it possible to serve customers faster while reducing call center costs. Before this wording was adopted, people experimented with the right sentence to say and the length of a pause before a second message, which stated, "Alternatively, please continue to hold."

The experiment then tested the optimal time before the second part of the message was played twice: for one second and then for five seconds. With the five-second option, 9 percent more customers visited the website than with the one-second option. The team then experimented with adding, "Avoid waiting on the line," which played during the five-second pause. These five words led to a further 6 percent increase in choosing the digital option.

They then experimented with a 10-second pause and played music. The outcome? Because people enjoyed the music, it did not improve the adoption rate of a digital option. The highest adoption results came from a five-second pause between the two statements with a prompt. As more customers used live chat and social media to connect to a service, call center volumes fell 8 percent in 2019.

- **Virtual Reality at Branches**

This experiment introduced virtual reality (VR) for customers. When they put on VR goggles, they were immersed into their desired lifestyle 20 years into the future so they could calculate how much money they needed to save for retirement. The experience guided them through four key expenditure lifestyle areas that included dining, transportation, travel, and household. They could then calculate the retirement funds they needed to achieve their desired quality of life and start working toward their goals.

- **Video Teller Machines (VTMs)**

In 2019, the bank rolled out Singapore's first video teller machines (VTMs). These machines provided a private booth for customers to do transactions through the machine. Alternatively, they could receive face-to-face assistance from a bank teller located in a central operations area rather than at a bank branch. The 24/7 VTMs are able, for example, to replace bank cards and security tokens.

Initially, the bank experimented with having young employees staff the VTMs, assuming the new technology would fit better with younger rather than older employees. But in fact, older staff who were accustomed to using Skype preferred to be the ones to support the VTMs.

- ***Sparks* Online Mini-series**

The bank's development of a culture of experimentation with an openness to failure led to the creation of *Sparks*.

If you haven't seen DBS's *Sparks* online yet, I suggest you watch it before reading on. It's available on Facebook or YouTube. This online miniseries, inspired by true customer stories, shares key messages to make the bank relevant in a social media world. In this way, the Marketing team is able to convey relevant stories in a touching manner.

By embracing the spirit of a start-up culture and a desire to experiment, the team pushed ahead with the idea, winning over Piyush's approval. Its carefully calculated gamble paid off wonderfully. Piyush even had a cameo appearance in season one, episode eight, while Sachin Tendulkar, a famous cricketer, was featured in seasons one and two.

This miniseries is an amazingly innovative way of showing the bank's personality and sharing its fundamental messaging (e.g., Fintech disruption, the work of DBS Foundation, prioritizing living over business, and more). Since *Sparks* was launched, DBS has set up its own in-house studio to produce it.

As Piyush explained, *Sparks* required a completely new way of thinking about marketing. It wasn't driven from the top down; rather, it came through the Marketing team. He noted the value of bringing content and social media together through *Sparks* to achieve strong branding.

The two seasons of *Sparks* have garnered 276,000 million views and 50 million engagements (likes, comments, or shares). It has also influenced close to 10 percent of the inquiries the bank has received online; for example, it generated 40 percent more visits to DBS's home page in 2020 over 2019. Because people think *Sparks* is cool, it's also helpful as a recruitment tool.

Sparks has been credited as an industry-first move. In its first year, the miniseries took home accolades for Best Film and Video in the Asia-Pacific Excellence Awards. In October 2017, it clinched the Gold Award in Digital Marketing at the global Efma-Accenture 2017 Distribution & Marketing Innovation Awards. This first-time win for DBS represented another creative way the bank has emphasized the importance of experimentation.

In 2018, as part of Singapore's 50-year celebration, Singapore Prime Minister Lee Hsien Loong was present to view the commissioned *Sparks: The Musical*, which paid tribute to the bank's pioneers and employees. Season 2 attracted more than 144 million views and helped generate twice the number of visits to DBS's website compared with season 1.

Sparks would never have received approval unless the bank had developed an experimental culture and openly took risks.

This demonstrates how bankers can challenge the status quo to go "above and beyond" when solving unusual customer problems. It also reflects the bank's commitment to understanding what matters to its customers while showing how banking can integrate seamlessly with everyday living.

2. Empowerment

DBS leaders cascaded the Digital Wave across their teams while empowering employees and encouraging experimentation in various ways. The following three case studies provide excellent examples.

- **POSB Smart Senior**

Employees in the Consumer bank in Singapore wanted to target two untapped markets: schools and the army. (In Singapore, army duty is compulsory for men, so the targeted population is relatively large.) During a meeting with a senior government official, the bank was told it was trying to tackle two of the most difficult areas in Singapore and would not succeed.

Nevertheless, the leaders empowered a team to start digitalizing the country's schools. This involved talking to the ministry of education and principals of schools as well as teachers, parents, children, and vendors. And that was just to get approval in one pilot school!

This tough challenge could have consumed too much time and energy. But the bank had adopted an experimentation mindset, and its leaders wanted to let "1,000 flowers bloom"—a Chinese expression that means "to plant many seeds of opportunity."

The idea of digitalization in schools quickly evolved into a program called Smart Buddy, as explained earlier. After its successful launch, a different government official called DBS to ask if it could do a similar program for the elderly. It would, for example, allow tracking of people with dementia if they wandered off and no one knew where they were.

The request to solve problems for the elderly led to creating POSB Smart Senior, the world's first holistic health and payment program developed for seniors. It features a new digital device, the POSB Smart Sleeve, that encompasses a variety of lifestyle functions such as transit, payments, fitness, and location-based tracking.

- **Call Center App Designed by Employees**

Designing the DBS call center app is a constructive example of how the bank empowered employees to improve operations.

In 2015, the Consumer call center identified five key customer pain points and then set about resolving them. The team built its own app to leverage open source tools and solve these pain points. The app helped create a community among all of the call center employees and integrate performance metrics so they could track and control their own performances.

The call center employees did not stop there. They built in their own rewards system.

The outcome? The app not only helped employees solve customers' pain points; it also built a sense of digital engagement early on and demonstrated what was possible in Making Banking Joyful. The app was then rolled out across the bank's other call centers.

This app has since evolved to include shift bidding. In the old system, employees were told what shift they had to take. That meant they had to be in the office to check the schedule and be present to negotiate any changes. Now, with this function on the app, employees can check their shift from home and place bids when they need to change shifts for a special event. The app responds on the same day, which the employees love.

- **Credit Card Annual Fee**

A common request in banking is for customers to ask for their credit card's annual fee to be waived. In response, the bank empowered the call center team to decide yes or no. As a result, the number of fees waived stayed consistent, but the service levels rose as customers received prompt replies rather than being told someone would get back to them.

In addition, when customers complained about small amounts even as low as one dollar, the call center had to go to the related business to obtain permission to solve the problem. Today, call center employees are empowered to correct customer changes up to $100. This change has improved employee engagement and pride because it allowed them to take corrective action on the spot.

These changes demonstrate and reinforce the trust the bank puts in its employees to Make Banking Joyful.

3. Awards to Encourage the Right Behaviors

As part of the employee journey, the bank has introduced various awards to encourage employees' right behaviors. Two of them are described here.

- **"iTQ" (I Thank You) Award**

This is an online peer-to-peer recognition program that made saying thank you to anyone across the bank (and across geographies) simple and autonomous—no approvals required.

Every employee had 2,000 iTQ points and was empowered to give 100 points at a time to a coworker through a digital portal. Whenever points were given, they were accompanied with a personal message linked to DBS's corporate values. Employees could then redeem the points they received by selecting from a wide range of benefits such as health and wellness activities.

- **Dare to Fail Award**

To reinforce a safe environment for taking risks without the fear of failure, DBS created the Dare to Fail award. This award gives positive recognition to those who achieved early successes when experimenting, and it has spurred employees to pursue new ideas. Piyush showcased the Dare to Fail award in town halls as a way to encourage the right behaviors. He also reviews new projects or programs every few months and showcases multiple successes and failures. Overall, about 10 percent of the experiments are adopted.

To reinforce a safe environment for taking risks without the fear of failure, DBS created the Dare to Fail award.

The five start-up culture characteristics—**A**gile, **B**e a learning organization, **C**ustomer obsessed, **D**ata driven, and **E**xperiment—are deeply embedded into the DNA of DBS.

While implementing the Digital Wave, leaders were conscious of the role they played in the communities where they had a presence. This led to the launch of the third wave—the Sustainability Wave.

Questions for Consideration

1. How can you create an environment that encourages the right actions to implement your digital transformation?
2. How does your culture need to change?
3. What needs to change in your employees' mindset to implement digital?
4. How can your organization reduce bureaucracy?
5. How can you make your meetings more efficient and effective?
6. What needs to happen for employees to be encouraged to experiment?
7. How can you create a culture of psychological safety?
8. What awards can you introduce to recognize failures?
9. How can agile be adopted across all functions and employee levels?
10. How can you create a data-first culture across the whole organization?
11. What governance needs to be in place for the use of data across the organization?
12. How do you ensure data is at the heart of strategic and operational decision-making?
13. What skills training do employees need to become more proficient in using data?

CHAPTER 20

The Sustainability Wave

Recently, DBS Bank changed its vision from being the best bank in the world (BBIW) to being the best bank for a better world (BBBW). Its leaders are striving to create a vision that is bigger than the bank itself. This change led to the launch of the Sustainability Wave—an initiative that focuses on inequality, new social norms, and the future of our planet. All of these issues are becoming increasingly crucial in the 21st century.

Through its Sustainability Wave, the bank aims to correct inequalities in the communities where it operates.

The New Vision

DBS leaders arrived at this new vision—being the best bank for a better world—by considering these key elements:

1. VUCA
2. Fault lines in socioeconomic situations
3. "Heroes vs. villains" framework for corporations

1. VUCA

VUCA has become a common business term to describe the Volatility, Uncertainty, Complexity, and Ambiguity organizations face. The term emerged from the U.S. Army during the Cold War—an era that generally spanned from the end of World War II to the 1991 dissolution of the Soviet Union.

Organizations constantly deal with VUCA-like events, both internally and externally, which are affecting them either negatively or positively. As DBS leaders recognized that the VUCA reality added complexity to their decision-making, they wanted to make decisions that were good both for the bank and the communities it operated in.

2. Fault Lines in Socioeconomic Situations

In 2018, Oxfam published this statement: "Inequality as a social, political and development issue has risen toward the top of public agendas, with its damaging impacts on social, environmental and economic sustainability and its link to poverty, insecurity, crime and xenophobia now widely demonstrated and acknowledged."[19] It begs the question "What is the best way to address this problem?"

After the Global Financial Crisis of 2008–9, the fault lines in socioeconomic situations became more visible. In addition, the tensions between those who "have" and those who "have not" rose. Occurring a few years after the Global Financial Crisis, the Occupy Wall Street movement highlighted the differences between those who held 1 percent of the world's wealth versus those who controlled 99 percent of it.

---

19 Emma Seery et al., "Even It Up: Time to End Extreme Inequality," Oxfam, accessed April 16, 2021, https://s3.amazonaws.com/oxfam-us/www/static/media/files/even-it-up-inequality-oxfam.pdf.

Then in 2020, the Covid-19 pandemic brought evidence of inequality to new heights, exposing the vulnerabilities of individuals, societies, and economies. Examples include the differences between emerging and developing countries in making available economic stimulus packages and a Covid-19 vaccine to their people.

> "The pandemic has accentuated socioeconomic fault lines within countries, compelling governments to direct more fiscal resources to the poor." – *Piyush (CEO)*[20]

Discussions on how to address fault lines in social economic situations were highlighted in 2020 with Simon Sinek publishing his book, *The Infinite Game.*[21]

For DBS, the aim became going beyond competing with its peers (a finite game) to constantly evolving and, in the process, creating something bigger: *the best bank for a better world* (an infinite game).

For DBS, the aim became going beyond competing with its peers (a finite game) to constantly evolving and, in the process, creating something bigger: *the best bank for a better world* (an infinite game).

DBS continually questions itself on whether banking has a big enough purpose while also recognizing ways to strive toward being the best bank for a better world. It recognizes that, as a bank, it has the ability to:

- Do real things for real people to enrich lives.

---

20 "Annual Report 2020," DBS, accessed April 16, 2021, page 12, https://www.dbs.com/annualreports/2020/index.html?pid=sg-group-pweb-investors-pdf-2020-stronger-together.

21 Simon Sinek, *The Infinite Game* (New York: Portfolio Penguin, 2020).

- Enable businesses to transform and grow.
- Make a difference by supporting communities.
- Be responsible to the society at large.

The strategic shift of creating a Sustainability Wave caused DBS leaders to step back and ask *who* and *what* they were working for—shareholders or stakeholders? This marks the debate between the virtues of "shareholder capitalism" and what is increasingly referred to as "stakeholder capitalism."

From a shareholder's perspective, it's an organization's responsibility to maximize the value that goes to shareholders. Therefore, the responsibility for societal good belongs to governments, which are better suited to that role than corporations.

DBS leaders recognized that the perceived trade-off between shareholder and stakeholder values boils down to a time frame issue. In the short term, there may be a perceived trade-off. But by believing a social license is needed to operate and the time frame is extended, then any conflict between the two disappears. By taking the long-term view, the right thing to do is to support multiple stakeholders that include shareholders. With that approach, there is no need to trade value for values.

The desire for organizations to move from working for *shareholders* to working for *stakeholders* required creating a new statement of purpose for organizations.

3. Heroes vs. Villains Framework for Corporations

Acknowledgment that the bank was moving in the right direction was reinforced when, in 2019, 181 CEOs in the United States formally signed the Statement on the Purpose of a Corporation.[22]

22 "Business Roundtable Redefines the Purpose of a Corporation to Promote 'An Economy That Serves All Americans,'" Business Roundtable, August 19, 2019, https://www.businessroundtable.org/business-roundtable-redefines-the-purpose-of-a-corporation-to-promote-an-economy-that-serves-all-americans.

With it, the CEOs committed their organizations to benefit more people than their shareholders; they promoted stakeholder interests to the same level of importance as shareholder interests.

The CEOs involved debated whether *purpose* always competes with *profit* or if the two can coexist. They agreed that while each individual organization serves its own corporate purpose, all of them share a fundamental commitment to all stakeholders. Specifically, these leaders stated their commitment to:

- Invest in their employees.
- Deliver value to their customers.
- Deal fairly and ethically with their suppliers.
- Support the communities in which they operate.
- Generate long-term value for shareholders.[23]

> "This new statement better reflects the way corporations can and should operate today." – *Alex Gorsky (Chairman of the Board and CEO of Johnson & Johnson)*[24]

Research has shown that organizations with a high level of purpose outperform the market by 5 to 7 percent, as noted by Claudine Gartenberg and George Serafeim in a 2019 *Harvard Business Review* article.[25] This is on par with organizations who operate with best-in-class governance and innovation.

DBS leaders have established the necessity for businesses to recognize the importance of being purpose driven. Instead of focusing only on short-term profits, they aim to create value for

---

23 Ibid.

24 Ibid.

25 Claudine Gartenberg and George Serafeim, "181 Top CEOs Have Realized Companies Need a Purpose Beyond Profit," *Harvard Business Review*, August 20, 2019, https://hbr.org/2019/08/181-top-ceos-have-realized-companies-need-a-purpose-beyond-profit.

the community at large. Also, they agree that business leaders need to recognize they need two licenses to operate: regulatory and civil society.

In the long term, civil society must believe the organization brings the right value—and that value will help them exist for generations.

> Instead of focusing only on short-term profits, they aim to create value for the community at large.

As they've demonstrated through every wave in the past decade, DBS leaders have continued to place significant effort, time, and energy toward successfully executing each wave, including the Sustainability Wave. Similarly, the idea of creating a better world has become deeply rooted in the psyche of DBS.

The Three Pillars of the Sustainability Program

To become a purpose-driven bank, the leadership team has identified three sustainable pillars to drive transformation. They are:

- Responsible banking
- Responsible business practices
- Creating social impact

1. Responsible Banking

The bank strives to deliver products and services that promote sustainable development while conducting its business in a fair and responsible manner. Here are some examples:

- The bank stopped financing coal-fired power plants in any market in 2019.

- DBS adopted responsible financing in its lending practices to support its customers in moving toward a more sustainable low-carbon business model. It also focused on improving customers' access to ESG (Environmental, Social, and Corporate Governance) investments. The bank recognized that financing customers who do not have the capacity or capability to mitigate ESG risks can be detrimental to the bank and society.
- Through its lending and capital market activities, bank leaders have focused on climate change and its necessary targets to encourage and support a low-carbon economy. Climate-related risks are considered part of the ESG risk assessment that the bank conducts on its customers.
- The bank's credit risk policy has incorporated principles and approaches to manage ESG issues. It has introduced sustainable financial products such as sustainability-linked loans that provide businesses with incentives to improve their environmental and social footprints. For example, in 2019, DBS partnered with PT Sumatera Timberindo Industry (a leading premium wooden furniture door manufacturer in Indonesia). Together, they created the first export financing sustainability-linked loan of its kind in Indonesia. Their loans were evaluated on their ability to obtain timber on raw materials from recognized sources. The interest rate was reduced for each shipment of raw material that was certified by the Forest Stewardship Council.
- Early successes in the Sustainability Wave included co-creating with HeveaConnect (a digital trading marketplace for natural rubber producers), an ecosystem platform to provide traceability and transparency in the rubber supply chain. DBS also collaborated with Agrocorp

(a leading integrated agricultural commodity and food solutions provider) to create a block chain trading platform that would provide greater efficiency, cost savings, and transparency to Agrocorp's supply chain participants.

- In general, bank leaders encourage customers to adopt environmental and social practices. Today, with any credit application, the bank has an RM check for ESG risk assessment for each borrower. It also conducts evaluations of its corporate clients, which may include a site visit or certification requirement.

In 2020, DBS's responsible banking highlights included the following:

- Increased its sustainable financing by more than 80 percent, with 50 sustainability financing deals amounting to $9.6 billion. The target is to reach $50 billion by 2024.
- Property developer and investment company Hongkong Land reached an agreement with DBS to convert an existing HK$1 billion (S$175.8 million) five-year revolving credit facility into a sustainability-linked loan.
- Eight to 10 percent of its AUM (total assets under management) are to be channeled into sustainable investments.
- As part of its efforts to help clients from key industries transition to a low-carbon economy, it introduced Sustainable and Transition Finance Framework and Taxonomy. This has been recognized as the world's first such framework by a bank.
- Championed a new Zero Food Waste campaign that reduced more than 200,000 kg of foodwaste as a result of raising awareness on this issue and redistributing excess food that would have been wasted.

- Closed $9.6 billion in sustainable financing transactions. This was up 81 percent from the previous year.
- The bank ranked first in Bloomberg's Asia league tables for green loans.
- Named to the Dow Jones Sustainability Index (Asia-Pacific) for the third consecutive year.
- Named to the FTSE4Good Global Index for the fourth consecutive year.

DBS has also focused on making finance accessible to those who did not have access. According to the World Bank, about 1.7 billion people worldwide do not have access to basic financial services. To serve this sector, DBS does not use traditional micro financing but its own digital finance platforms to make financing more accessible. This includes, for example, using AI, mobile platforms, and block chain. Its digital finance platforms allow for a lower cost of transactions, easier acquisition of customers, and a greater reach to underserved segments.

In total, the bank has provided more than $15 billion in responsible financing for sustainable-linked loans, renewable and clean energy–related loans, and green loans.

Many of the initiatives noted earlier in this book have been driven partly by the Sustainability Wave, including:

- Smart Buddy is the world's first in-school savings and payments for children worn on their wrists. It helps them develop their financial awareness.
- DBS's digiPortfolio, the in-house hybrid human-robo investment solution, supports the democratization of wealth and investment.

In total, the bank has provided more than $15 billion in responsible financing for sustainable-linked loans, renewable and clean energy–related loans, and green loans. Green loans are made exclusively to finance eligible green projects in energy efficiency, pollution prevention, and similar areas.

2. Responsible Business Practices

DBS Bank aims to improve its business operations by creating stronger employee engagement and collaborative efforts in sustainable procurement. Its focus: *To do the right thing with its most important resource—its people.* Two examples are creating the Workforce Transformation Award and introducing Anytime Feedback, which allows employees to request advice on how to grow and improve in their jobs.

In addition, training in ECG is provided to employees to better understand responsible financing. For example, RMs and CRMs were specifically given training on human trafficking and modern-day slavery. The aim was to raise awareness of emerging issues and to enhance their employees' understanding of their early warning signals and relevance to the community.

To do the right thing with its most important resource—its people.

The bank's responsible business practices include ensuring employees can develop their skills by investing in upscaling and rescaling to gradually build an open culture.

The bank also embraces gender and culture diversity. For example, it introduced a program in India specifically for female colleagues. Called EmpowerHer, it supports women's learning and growth. It also launched iHealth@DBS program to encourage employees to live well, eat well, stay well, and save well. The bank also encourages employees to voluntarily participate in sustainable events. In India, for example, employees volunteered to plant 200 saplings of Rhizophora mangle (red mangrove) species. It also supports initiatives to reduce its environmental footprint.

> "Sustainability was always around people, planet, and profit. I just think for the longest time we've forgotten about the people." – *Mikkel (Chief Sustainability Officer)*[26]

3. Creating Social Impact

The bank aims to become a "force of good" by supporting social enterprises, businesses with a double bottom line (a second bottom line measures the organization's performance in terms of positive social impact) and giving back to the communities in which it operates.

In conjunction with Singapore's 50th year as a nation, the bank launched its DBS Foundation in 2014 starting with a $50 million fund. This signaled the bank's commitment to addressing the region's evolving social needs. Specifically, it has been championing social entrepreneurship and encouraging businesses to strive for goodness. The goal was always to build a more inclusive Asia.

The Foundation built on work done in DBS Social Enterprise Package—an industry launched in 2009. The DBS Social Enterprise Package provides SEs (Social Enterprises) with a low-cost banking solution, such as zero-minimum balance for account opening and unsecured loans at preferential rates.

Programs range from venture challenges, learning forums, grant support, and financing to skilled volunteer mentoring. In this way, the bank is championing social entrepreneurship—that

26 *ESG Insider*, an S&P Global podcast, accessed April 16, 2021, https://podcasts.apple.com/us/podcast/esg-insider-a-podcast-from-s-p-global/id1475521006.

is, businesses that not only have a *profitable financial* bottom line but also a *social impact* bottom line. By addressing social concerns, it plays a critical role in solving a myriad of social problems.

Specifically, the DBS Foundation:

- Advocates for social enterprises through competitions, challenges, boot camps, workshops, and learning forums
- Nurtures promising social enterprises through grant funding, capacity building, and mentorship
- Integrates social enterprises into the culture and operations of the bank

In 2019, the Foundation launched its inaugural DBS Foundation Social Impact Prize in partnership with Singapore Management University. The prize aims to identify sustainable, scalable, and enterprising business solutions that address crucial social problems and make cities of the future more inclusive, healthier, and greener.

The Foundation has supported more than 60 SEs (Social Enterprises) in the region with over $5.5 million in grant funding, deployed in areas such as healthcare, social inclusion, environment protection, waste management, and food sustainability. Eight DBS Foundation-supported social entrepreneurs were named in the 2018 and 2019 *Forbes* "30 under 30" lists. In 2019, Singapore's president recognized the Foundation for its efforts in supporting social enterprises tackling various issues.

However, the journey to create responsible business practices has not been easy. This has been especially true when a conflict in pursuing certain sustainable development goals is evident. For example, the net impact assessment is essential in determining if an industry creates an overall positive or negative impact. But, again, this is not easy to discern, as no consistent measures are readily available.

Still, DBS has taken the initiative to develop an impact measurement framework that allows it to see the effects of its lending. In one example, imposing stringent ESG requirements on its palm oil customers led to reducing environmental and social problems. And Sustainability Wave initiatives were strongly put to the test in the way DBS responded to the Covid-19 pandemic, as discussed in the next chapter.

Recognition for Its Sustainability Efforts

DBS's Sustainability Wave efforts have already been recognized by being named the inaugural winner of the "Social Enterprise Champion of the Year (Corporation)" and included in the Bloomberg Gender-Equality Index (four consecutive years), FTSE4Good Global Index (four consecutive year), and Dow Jones Sustainability Index (three consecutive years).

The bank has adopted the Equator Principles,[27] which links due diligence related to finance to environmental and social challenges, and it adheres to due diligence processes in accordance with International Finance Corporation Performance Standards.

27 Equator Principles, website, accessed April 16, 2021, https://equator-principles.com/.

CHAPTER 21

Covid-19 Pandemic Response

The worldwide Covid-19 pandemic has once again shone the light on the role banks play in society.

As a testament to being a force for good, DBS Bank rolled out a series of support measures for individuals, businesses, communities, and employees during the initial year of the Covid-19 pandemic. Its primary focus was to provide comfort, solace, and support as it released a strong commitment.

The bank's key supporting initiatives centered around providing support to retail customers, providing cash flow support to corporate customers, leveraging its digital solutions to assist customers, standing together with its employees, doing its part for the community, and providing operational resilience and telecommuting at scale.

This commitment to customers was supported by these initiatives:

1. The DBS Stronger Together Fund
2. Being a responsible member of the community
3. Beefed-up support for social enterprises with cash flow and skills training

1. The DBS Stronger Together Fund

The DBS Stronger Together Fund was a $10.5 million fund set up to assist communities hard hit by Covid-19 across the Asia region. The fund provided about 4.5 million meals and care packs to those affected. It also supported the procurement of diagnostic test kits, personal protective equipment, and other medical supplies to help in the fight against Covid-19. DBS leaders showed their belief that by standing together, everyone could overcome this crisis and emerge stronger.

The bank responded in its markets in various ways, including:

- In Singapore, it matched dollar-for-dollar donations to provide more than 700,000 meals for elderly people, low-income families, and migrant workers.
- In Hong Kong, it provided resources for local charities to expand their outreach programs to the elderly and vulnerable communities.
- In China, it provided about 1.7 million meals to affected communities over 12 months.
- In India, it partnered with NGOs to scale up public health infrastructure and sponsor free tests for the underprivileged.
- In Indonesia, it donated medical supplies and test kits to address the current shortage.
- In Taiwan, it donated 50,850 food packs to those in need, with all products purchased from social enterprises.

To help organizations remain competitive, the bank upskilled its clients' business capabilities online. For example, its Online

SME Academy[28] features actionable insights by industry practitioners while offering subjects such as innovation, branding, trade finance, cash management the digital way, and social media engagement.

Like many other organizations during the pandemic, DBS customers who had resisted adopting digital interfaces turned to them. The bank, for example, had four times the number of people over 60 who became willing to adopt digital channels due to the pandemic.

2. Being a Responsible Member of the Community

Bank leaders recognized their deep responsibility to step up and provide financial relief to needy people during these difficult times. DBS played its part by:

- Providing cash flow support—one of the single biggest needs during the pandemic.
- Lowering the cost of lending—for example, by allowing eligible customers to convert credit card loans (which draw annual interest in the 20+ percent range) to one in which the effective interest rate is capped at 8 percent.
- Providing new kinds of lending to marginal borrowers. For example, the Singapore government stepped in to cover risk up to 80 or 90 percent on some SME loans. This dramatically improved the bank's ability to give loans to marginal borrowers. Under this program, DBS approved more than 1,200 loans worth over $1 billion.

28 "Online SME Academy," DBS.com, accessed April 16, 2021, https://www.dbs.com.sg/sme/businessclass/sme-online-academy.page?pk_source=typed&pk_medium=direct&pk_campaign=bookmarked.

- Helping customers conduct their banking digitally. This became imperative during lockdown periods when companies outside of essential services had to function through telecommuting. With employees working from home, it simply made no sense to still have to go to the branch to carry out banking transactions. For example, DBS employees helped customers digitalize their trade finance, which had heavily depended on physical documents.
- Working with two Singapore tech start-ups, Oddle and FirstCom, DBS supported its food and beverage customers in establishing an online presence through digital shopfront, e-menus, and social media presence.
- Helping change payment methods for some of the large government agencies in Singapore. Within the first month of the lockdown in Singapore, they wanted to reduce the number of checks, so they reached out to DBS to change their payment method.

• Account Opening for Migrant Workers

A challenging issue that arose in Singapore was the rapid spread of the Covid-19 pandemic through migrant workers living in dormitories. Before the pandemic, this relatively small segment was not a focus for the bank. However, the need for migrant workers to quarantine created a banking issue because this group had a habit of sending cash to their families through physical bank branches.

To provide a digital solution, DBS worked with the Singapore government and opened over 40,000 foreign digital accounts over a weekend so these workers could have access to digital banking services during quarantine. With the assistance of the

Ministry of Manpower, DBS people were able to digitally conduct KYC (Know Your Customer) and populate the account details. Once the workers were electronically notified that their accounts were open, they could do remittance through a bank app known as POSB Jolly. The app has five language options to choose from: English, Bahasa Indonesia, Bengali, Chinese, and Tamil. Over half a million downloads of this app have taken place!

To provide a digital solution, DBS worked with the Singapore government and opened over 40,000 foreign digital accounts over a weekend so these workers could have access to digital banking services during quarantine.

3. Beefed-up Support for Social Enterprises with Cash Flow and Skills Training

DBS increased access to financing to more than 360 social enterprises (SEs) in Singapore to help alleviate cash flow woes and to protect jobs in sector. The DBS Foundation pledged $500,000 in additional funding for SEs regionwide, and the bank provided access to business and digital transformation courses at no charge.

Even months after Covid-19 emerged, the bank has kept supporting its customers with relief measures such as account-related fees, various credit card loans, further study assistance insurance, and an online video-based license for kids.

- **The Last Mile—the Final 10 percent**

As a result of responding to this pandemic, the bank realized its customers could not complete all activities they needed online. Even though 90 percent of banking activity was already in place digitally, it raced against time to focus on last-mile processes so both retail and SME customers could bank in the safety of their own homes and enjoy uninterrupted banking services. When the pandemic hit, the bank was well positioned to pivot to digital and contactless services and solutions.

> "The bank was able to respond quickly because of its modern technology stack, enterprise adoption of Agile, and two-in-a-box platform." – *Jimmy (Chief Information Officer)*

- **DBS Employees**

From the start, the bank told its employees there would be no layoffs arising from the Covid-19 pandemic. This was particularly well received among branch employees, given that 50 percent of the branches in Singapore were closed due to the lockdown.

Being digitally driven enabled the bank to respond quickly to internal challenges from the Covid-19 pandemic. For example, it leveraged data analytics and AI to pull together data (from turnstile taps, outlook, Wi-Fi access, meeting rooms, etc.) and create a contact tracing solution within 48 hours. They were able to implement the first solution quickly because of clear project objectives and support across various teams. It was also able to promptly overcome security risks for employees working at home and became better positioned to support employees in the radically new working environment. Also, over 90 percent of employees were already using laptops before the pandemic, which made working from home easier.

DBS supported its employees through these challenging times by:

- Continuing full pay, including branch staff members unable to perform their duties because of temporary branch closures during lockdown.
- Restructuring to allow as many as 90 percent of the employees to work at home during the height of the pandemic. Piyush led the way by immediately working from home to set the example.
- Supporting employees to adopt new ways of working by providing tips for starting new routines and working from home. Virtual team meals and group fitness exercises were organized.
- Guiding leaders on how to boost team morale and engage teams remotely. For example, at the start of virtual calls was a "check in" when participants rated their emotional health on a scale of one to 10.
- Launching a monthly "happiness challenge" in which people in different departments demonstrated how they stayed happy.
- Providing e-learning programs for employees to upskill amid the lull in work activity.
- Ensuring security code controls as stringent for employees as they were for customers using a strategy called "Inside is the new Outside."

At the height of the pandemic, the bank committed to hiring more than 2,000 people in Singapore.

- **Virtual Customer Journeys**

How would the bank continue to conduct customer journeys during the pandemic? Before, employees got involved in a war room using whiteboards and Post-It notes. But with everybody working remotely, the bank launched Project Lemonade, a virtual customer journey workshop. After approaching other organizations to identify best practices for conducting virtual workshops, leaders redesigned the existing customer journey workshop to be virtual. They accomplished this in only seven days!

- **Soul of the Organization**

From the first month of the lockdown, bank leaders had turned their focus to the soft side of the business.

Toward the end of 2020, Piyush reflected that one of the biggest challenges during the pandemic was keeping the cultural soul of the organization together. Dealing with the pandemic's psychological impact and keeping teams and people together was his focus. Allowing people into bank systems from home became necessary.

Toward the end of 2020, Piyush reflected that one of the biggest challenges during the pandemic was keeping the cultural soul of the organization together.

To manage the loneliness of being home all day alone in front of a screen, the bank launched a program called Together. In this program, everyone had a buddy for organized relax times in which they played virtual games or had remote social sessions in the evening.

In the middle of 2020, the bank created a task force to think about the future of work. It identified the need to pivot toward a hybrid working model. As a result of the pandemic, employees now have the ability to work both in the office and from home. In fact, up to 40 percent of an employee's time can be working from home.

The task force also identified that, for the future of work, the agile squads needed to be nimbler. So, the bank continues to accelerate its transition from conventional functional departments to project-specific, data-driven squads made up of members from different functions with relevant areas of expertise. In addition, the task force identified a need to continue redesigning work in collaboration spaces. So the bank continues to reconfigure Joy Spaces, its activity-based workspaces. In its Singapore headquarters, it has also launched a 5,000-square-foot Living Lab to blend the best of physical and virtual workspace configurations.

DBS has continued to emphasize the importance of nurturing its culture. For example, new employees must spend time at the office to build their social capital. And any employees not performing as expected receive coaching in the office.

To support employees who need flexible work arrangements, the bank offers a job-sharing scheme, which divides a typical full-time job between two employees who share the responsibilities.

The extraordinary steps DBS Bank took to support its stakeholders during the pandemic will undoubtfully produce enormous benefits in the future.

To act less like a bank and more like a tech organization, DBS had asked itself, "What would Jeff (Bezos) do?" The question now being asked in other organizations is:

"What would the World's Best Bank do?"

Appendix

A. *World's Best Bank* Platform

To support the experience from this digital transformation there are a number of interactive activities presented in this platform.

Activities on the *World's Best Bank* Platform

1. Keynote: The Story and Lessons from a World Class Digital Transformation

www.bridgesconsultancy.com/keynotes/dbs-bank-journey-becoming-best-digital-now-best-bank-world-keynote

This keynote shares how DBS Bank transformed from a traditional bank to the world's best bank by leveraging digitalization. It highlights how the bank created a 29,000-employee start-up, transformed its technology core, and became customer obsessed—the bank's three strategic principles for digital transformation. Woven throughout the keynote is also what the bank did differently to implement its strategy and features best practices from Speculand's book, *World's Best Bank.*

2. Execution Box Set

www.bridgesconsultancy.com/product-category/books

Speculand's trilogy book set guides leaders on how to overcome the high failure rate of digital transformations. Books included in the set are:

- *The "HOW" to: Excellence in Execution – How to Implement Your Strategy:*

Equips business leaders with the components and "how to" needed to be successful in strategy execution.

- *The "WORKBOOK": 182 Questions for Digital Execution – Strategy Implementation Starts with the Right Questions*

Prepares leaders to develop a comprehensive execution plan during their organization's strategy planning by asking the right questions stated in this book.

- *The in-depth "CASE STUDY": World's Best Bank – A Strategic Guide to Digital Transformation*

Explains how a whole organization digitally transformed with key learnings and best practices that are easy to adopt .

3. DBS: Digital transformation to Best Bank in the World – Harvard-listed case study

www.bridgesconsultancy.com/research-case-study/research

Transfers digital transformation lessons through case study teaching, and it's ideal for educating your team.

4. Video Vault – sample:

https://www.youtube.com/watch?v=lYsDbjP98fw

Contains 32 three-minute videos with key lessons from DBS bank digital transformation. As well as the 32 videos, you receive the 19-page video vault guide that explains, for teaching, the key message, the essential question or best practice, and the page reference to the book for more information.

5. 40 Digital Best Practices Benchmark

www.bridgesconsultancy.com/
40-digital-best-practices-benchmark

Allows assessment of an organization against the key building blocks of digital transformation in four sections: Strategy, Technology, Customer, and Culture.

6. Digital Maturity Index

www.bridgesconsultancy.com/product/
digital-maturity-index-purchase-offer-as-facilitators-instrument/#tab-description

Allows individuals to assess their digital maturity.

7. Course: DBS Making Banking Joyful

www.bridgesconsultancy.com/bridges-courses/
dbs-bank-transformation-to-
best-digital-bank-in-the-world

This absorbing, informative, and enlightening one-day workshop or four virtual modules explains in depth how DBS achieved this remarkable transformation to become the world's best bank. It features exclusive insights, best practices, and stories.

This course is for leaders looking to understand how to be successful in digital transformation. They will learn from one of the leading digital transformations in the world. Its content provides a strategic guide, provocative questions, and best practices.

The course includes the Harvard-listed university DBS case study (co-authored by Speculand) and two pre-course assessments.

8. Strategy Implementation Online Course & Certification

www.strategyimplementationinstitute.org

Digital transformation involves not only the adoption and integration of technology but also the implementation of the strategy. To support employees and set them up for success, this three-month, part-time, online course provides the tools, tips, and techniques and the knowledge to succeed in strategy implementation. See next page for more details.

B. Strategy Implementation Institute

For those passionate about strategy implementation

The Strategy Implementation Institute (Institute) was founded in 2019 by Antonio Nieto-Rodriguez and Robin Speculand, two global thought leaders who share a passion to develop people to be implementation professionals.

The Institute brings people together from around the world who are passionate about implementation and is creating an online community for them to learn, share, and grow. It recognizes that implementing strategy is a rare and highly appreciated skill set that sets apart the most influential and successful leaders in business.

People with the skill to implement strategy are in high demand from organizations all around the world. This is especially true at a time when strategies are being formed and implemented at a more rapid pace than ever before. To meet this increasing demand for skilled implementors, the Institute offers:

1. Membership to the online community – complementary for the first year when purchased with the Strategy Implementation Professional online course
2. Strategy Implementation Professional (SIP) online course – a seven-course module open to everyone. It is based on the Institute's propriety body of knowledge and the Strategy Implementation Roadmap© (SIR), which provides a step-by-step guide on how to implement strategy.
3. Online Professional exam and certification in partnership with APMG International

4. Online Fellowship course and certification – with minimum two years SIP accreditation and membership

Visit: www.strategyimplementationinstitute.org

C. Award-Winning Bank

Since its founding 50 years ago, DBS has always had a history of trailblazing and innovating. Its digital leadership has been honored as an organization that leads the way, not only in Asia but around the world.

In a first for a Singapore and Asian bank, DBS Bank has overtaken larger, more established banks to be named "Best Bank in the World." The prestigious top award was first conferred to DBS by *Global Finance* in its "World's Best Global Banks 2018 Awards."

In 2016 and 2018, DBS was named the "World's Best Digital Bank" and "World's Best SME Bank" in 2018 by *Euromoney*. In addition, it has been named "Safest Bank in Asia" by *Global Finance* for nine consecutive years (2009 to 2020).

DBS leaders attribute their progress to every one of their customers and employees in the region. Their belief in DBS's success has inspired them to lead the way in shaping the future of banking in Asia.

Awards and Accolades Won

- World's Best Bank – *Euromoney* 2021
- World's Best Digital – *Euromoney* 2021
- Global Most Innovative in Digital Banking – *The Banker* 2021
- World's Best Bank – *Euromoney* 2019
- Best Bank in the World – *Global Finance* 2018 and 2020
- Global Bank of the Year – *The Banker* 2018
- Top 10 Business Transformations of the Last Decade – *Harvard Business Review*
- Global Innovator – Gold

- World's Best Bank for SMEs
- SME Bank of the Year – Global (Platinum Winner) by Global SME Finance (International Finance Corporation)
- Cash Management Global Best Service – Overall: #1 by *Euromoney*
- #1 Behind the Login Experience by MyPrivateBanking
- Best Private Bank for Innovation – PWM/The Banker
- Efma – Accenture
- CIO100 Honoree – CIO
- FTSE4Good Global Index – FTSE Russell
- Dow Jones Sustainability Index (Asia-Pacific) – S&P Dow Jones Indices/RobecoSAM
- Regional Best Employer, Asia-Pacific – Kincentric
- Bloomberg Gender-Equality Index (since 2018) – Bloomberg
- Most Innovative Private Bank in the World – Global Finance
- CIO50 ASEAN – CIO
- Project Finance Advisory House of the Year, Asia-Pacific – The Asset
- Best in Treasury & Working Capital: SMEs, Asia-Pacific – The Asset
- Social Enterprise Champion of the Year (Corporation) – President's Challenge/
- Singapore Corporate Governance Award (Big Cap) – Securities Investors Association (Singapore)
- Business Leadership in Sustainability – Singapore Green Building Council –
- Special Recognition Award: Excellence in Human Capital Management – Singapore Corporate Awards

D. Glossary

AML – Anti Money Laundering

API – Application Programming Interface

Cash Outs – no cash is available in an ATM

Cloud Native – an approach to building and running scalable applications that leverages APIs and micro-services

Continuous Integration, Continuous Delivery – (CICD)

Data instrumentation – measure, monitor, and control a process by providing real-time knowledge of customers' journeys

Culture by Design – how you start by looking at your future state

DDOM - Data Driven Operating Model

DFD – Design for digital

DFNO – Design for no ops

DFD – Design for data

DevOps – the union of people, process, and products to enable continuous delivery of value to end users[29]

DigiFY – a mobile learning platform and online course intended to transform the company's bankers into digital bankers

4Ds – Discover, Define, Develop, and Deliver (not the lottery in Singapore)

Ecosystem – bringing together entities in disparate industries to create new offerings or capture value that individual organizations or sectors may not be capable of creating on their own

Future of Work – the pain points employees face every day

29 Sam Guckenheimer, "What Is DevOps" Microsoft.com, January 4, 2018, https://docs.microsoft.com/en-us/azure/devops/learn/what-is-devops.

GPU – Graphical Process Units

GANDALF – putting the "D" (DBS) in Google, Amazon, Netflix, Apple, LinkedIn, and Facebook

GTS – Global Transactions Services

HCD – Human Centered Design

IBG – Institutional Banking Group

ITSS – IT Shared Services

Kanban Boards – visuals used in the agile approach to show workflow

KPIs – Key Performance Indicators

MC2 – Management Committee two down from Piyush

MOJO

MO is the Meeting Owner

JO is the Joyful Observer

MVP – Minimal Viable Product

N=1 – providing an experience that's unique to the customer based on data

PIE – Project Improvement Initiatives

Platform – a set of applications, with a set of people with a joint budget to deliver a joint strategy (different from an Ecosystem Platform)

POC – Participate, Orchestrate, Create

PURE – Purposeful, Unsurprising, Respectful, and Explainable

QIRA – Quantum Image Recognition Application

RAPID – Real-time API with DBS

RED – Respectful, Easy to Deal With, and Dependable

RM – Relationship Manager

RPA – Robotic Processing Automation

Scrum – an agile way to manage projects

SME – Small Medium Enterprise

SOP – Standard Operating Procedures

Squads – small groups with a clear objective and short timeline

Stand-ups – short update sessions with no one sitting down

STP – Straight-Through Processing

Toil – the kind of work tied to running a production service that tends to be manual, repetitive, automatable, tactical, devoid of enduring value, and that scales linearly as a service grows[30]

T & M – Treasury and Markets

Tom (traditional) and Dave (digital) – way to refer to customers

Tribes – agile terminology for the name given to a collection of squads working together

YFP – Your Financial Profile

30 Vivek Raul, "Chapter 5: Eliminating Toil," *SRE*, (Sebastopol, CA: O'Reilly Media, 2017), https://landing.google.com/sre/sre-book/chapters/eliminating-toil/.

Acknowledgments

The initial idea for *World's Best Bank* started in 2018. Considerable time was then invested in researching, preparing, and writing DBS Bank's digital transformation story. The manuscript was completed at the start of 2020, but due to the global pandemic, I decided to postpone publishing the book. At the end of 2020, I not only updated the manuscript but added the final two chapters on sustainability and Covid-19.

Writing and publishing *World's Best Bank* has been a lengthy journey that required support and assistance to make it a reality. Let me acknowledge those who have taken this journey with me.

Most important, I'd like to thank GraceKelly, my wife, for the patience she has shown being married to an author (and entrepreneur) and given the weeks and years I have spent working on this manuscript.

I would like to thank Ron Kaufman, my friend and mentor for over a quarter of a century. His guidance on the direction of this book and his eye for detail in developing the cover added tremendous value.

It has been my pleasure to work with Barbara McNichol, my editor for over 15 years. Once again, we've collaborated on editing this manuscript from start to finish. As it evolved, Barbara enhanced my writing with her feedback. I continue to learn from her and appreciate her detailed eye and recommendations throughout the book. Our best man, Gary Berman, has an excellent eye for detail when reading and he was kind enough to proofread this manuscript and provide recommendations. Thank you to Michel Sznajer for once again providing initial feedback.

David Isaacs is a friend and marketing specialist I'd like to thank for our numerous conversations about the book's positioning. Our discussions led me to developing a platform for this book rather than selling it as a single product.

Thank you to Pam Nordberg who assisted with the proofreading. Also, my thanks to Rick Chappell who worked with me on the cover design and to Tony Bonds for his attention to detail in designing and uploading the manuscript.

My most significant thank you goes to you for purchasing this book and participating in the platform experience.

Made in the USA
Coppell, TX
12 May 2023

16713853R00125